Name _____

Sneaky Spelling Secrets

All of the sixth graders at Dukwilma School have been studying hard for the big spelling bee against Dailey School. The big bee takes place in just one week. Jack and David are learning how to spell words like "phosphorylase" and "photoautotrophic." They want to be ready.

Arnold, on the other hand, isn't studying at all. Instead, he has decided to be extra nice to Patty Peters, a sixth grader at Dailey School. Patty's dad is the judge of the spelling bee, and he has the list of spelling words for the big bee. Arnold has decided to woo his way to that list!

Every day after school, Arnold rides his bike to Dailey School. Then he carries Patty's books to the bus for her. After that, Arnold rides his bike as fast as he can to Patty's bus stop where he waits to carry her books home for her. At Patty's house, Arnold is extra friendly to her mom, who thinks Arnold is adorable.

One day while Arnold was at Patty's house, Patty's mom asked him to watch their house for a minute while she and Patty ran next door to find their cat. Arnold gladly said yes. It was the perfect time for him to snoop in Patty's dad's office to find the list of spelling words.

Check.

Arnold could have . . .

☐ found the list and taken it.   ☐ asked Patty's dad for the list.

☐ gotten caught looking for the list.   ☐ studied hard like everyone else.

Write.

If Arnold found the list, write what he might have done with it. _____

_____

Underline.

Chances are most of Arnold's honest friends would have . . .

    not wanted to see the list.   asked Arnold to give the list back.

    taken the list to study it.   told Patty not to trust Arnold.

Write.

What do you think would happen if all the Dukwilma sixth graders saw the list, won the spelling bee,

and were caught cheating? _____

_____

•SOMETHING EXTRA•

Write down three of the longest words you have ever seen. Learn to spell them.

Dancing Dilemma

It was finally here! The sixth grade students at Dukwilma had waited a long time for the annual Dandy Dukwilma Dance. Everyone in sixth grade was going. All the girls had new outfits to wear, and even the boys weren't complaining about having to dress up. Miss Freed was going to be there with her boyfriend, Sam Spacey.

One reason why the sixth graders were so excited about the dance was because the dance was almost canceled. Last year, a group of sixth grade boys let snakes loose in the gym during the dance. They hid them outside in boxes under the bushes. Then, saying they were warm from dancing, the boys went outside, smuggled in the snakes, and let them loose. Lots of the students screamed and even some of the teachers were afraid. The principal said there would never be another Dandy Dukwilma Dance.

But this new group of sixth graders, for the most part, is very responsible. Arnold and some of his friends are the exceptions. The students promised that everyone would behave and convinced the principal to let them have the dance.

This was the big night and everyone was behaving well. The dance was going great. Then, all of a sudden, the lights went out. The music stopped. Some students began to scream while Arnold and his friends snickered in a corner.

Write.

What do you think happened? Who do you think was responsible? Why? _____

_____

_____

_____

_____

Check.

If Arnold and his friends caused the lights to go off and the music to stop . . .

☐ there could be a dance on a different night.

☐ the dance could be forbidden.

☐ they could be in big trouble.

☐ there could be snakes in the gym.

Circle.

What probably happened was . . .

a fuse was blown.

snakes ate the lights and the music cords.

Arnold and his friends shut off the electricity.

the principal turned everything off.

•SOMETHING EXTRA•

Write about a time you thought someone had done something wrong and later you learned they had not been responsible.

Name _____

Must We Move?

Donald is upset. He is doing well in school, he's captain of a baseball team, he sold the most boxes of candy in the sixth-grade candy competition, and he has great friends. So why is he sad?

Donald's father is a professional football player. He was just offered an incredible contract with another team. This means the family would have to move. Donald is excited for his dad since his dad is getting older and probably doesn't have many more years left to play. At the same time, however, this is the first time Donald has lived anywhere for more than three years, and he really likes Dukwilma.

Donald's dad likes the offer of a ten-year contract, an increase in salary, and a position as a starting player. But he isn't sure if he should take it. He likes Dukwilma, his wife and children are happy here, and he has seriously thought of giving up football to start his own sporting goods business. He has invested his money wisely, so the salary isn't an issue. What should he do?

Check.

Donald thinks he will probably have to move because . . .

☐ his dad is the boss and he wants to go.

☐ his dad can play for ten more years.

☐ his family doesn't like Dukwilma.

☐ his dad can make a lot more money.

Underline.

Donald will probably . . .

adjust well if he moves.

play baseball again if he moves.

find new friends.

fail his classes at the new school.

Match.

move   Dad will make more money.

stay   The family is happy.

Dad is considering starting his own business.

Dad will get to play ten more years of football.

Foreign Friends

Kim and her parents and three brothers have decided to host an exchange student for a year. They had to supply lots of information about themselves so that they could be matched to a student with interests similar to theirs. They now have to decide between two students. Help them decide by reading the information on the two students below.

Corinne — French

- loves cats, dogs, rabbits
- loves hiking, camping, fishing, skiing, waterskiing, cycling
- loves small children
- has two brothers and one sister
- likes to cook and try new foods
- doesn't like to read or study
- will share a room
- wants to travel all over the U.S. to see the sights

Bruno — German

- loves reading and writing
- allergic to animals
- an only child
- doesn't like small children
- likes to watch TV, play video games, draw, play chess
- doesn't like to cook
- won't share a room
- wants to know well the family he stays with and become familiar with American culture

Write.
List Corinne and Bruno's similarities. _____
_____
_____
List Corinne and Bruno's differences. _____
_____
_____

Check.
If Kim's family chooses Corinne, they probably . . .

☐ do a lot of outdoor activities.   ☐ have animals.

☐ watch a lot of TV.   ☐ want to travel.

Underline.
If Kim's family chooses Bruno, they probably . . .

have no pets.   have a spare bedroom.   do a lot of outdoor activities.   don't have small children.

•SOMETHING EXTRA•
In which country would you want to be an exchange student? Why?

Morning Blues

Jackie is very grouchy on the mornings she has school. She hates to hear the music blaring from her clock radio each morning because that means it's time to get up. Jackie usually hits "snooze" at least three times. Her mother almost always has to drag her out of bed.

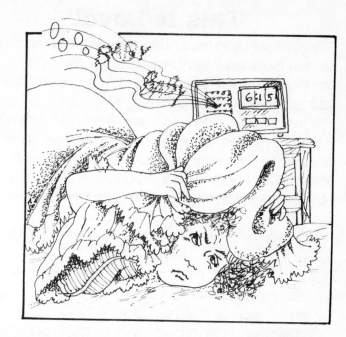

When Jackie has had her shower and brushed her teeth, she is awake but does not feel like talking. Miss Freed is lucky if Jackie even says "hello" when she arrives.

Jackie usually perks up by 9:30 when math class starts. She loves math. Actually, Jackie does well in all her classes and works hard to make good grades. She also has lots of friends. Jackie is always sharing with others and is good at including everyone in games.

When Jackie gets home from school, she is all smiles. She usually plays with her little sister Janie for a while. Then she plays with her friends before helping her mother prepare dinner. When her dad gets home, Jackie enthusiastically laughs as she tells him about her day.

After dinner, Jackie's family usually goes for a walk or plays a board game. Then Jackie does her homework and gets ready for bed. The problem is, however, that when it's time for bed, Jackie doesn't want to go to sleep. She begs her parents to let her stay up. They invariably say no, so Jackie goes to bed and usually lies there thinking for a long time before she falls asleep.

Check.

Jackie is . . .

☐ a morning person. ☐ always grouchy. ☐ usually considerate of others.

☐ a night person. ☐ studious. ☐ nice only when she wants to be.

Write.

How is Jackie a nice person? _____

_____

Underline.

Jackie dislikes . . .

music.   talking in the morning.   getting up for school.   school.

Write.

List some things you and Jackie have in common. _____

_____

•SOMETHING EXTRA•

Are you a morning or a night person? Explain.

This Is Love!

Miss Freed is in love. Things have really gotten serious between her and Sam Spacey. Of course, no one is perfect, but Miss Freed thinks Sam is pretty close to it.

Sam loves to go out to eat. Miss Freed thinks this is great because she hates to cook. They always go to fancy restaurants to eat fine food. Sometimes Miss Freed would enjoy a hamburger and French fries, but Sam always wants the best.

Having the best is fine with Miss Freed, but she thinks Sam sometimes goes too far. For instance, he never buys anything on sale because he thinks sale items are defective. And he only shops at the best stores.

Sam is also a kind person — almost too kind for Miss Freed. He will go out of his way to help anyone or anything. Once he stopped to help a dog that had been hit by a car. He took the dog, a stray, to a vet and paid $400 to cover the medical exenses. He was two hours late picking up Miss Freed for her parents' anniversary party.

Miss Freed feels she really shouldn't complain about Sam because he is such a good person. She enjoys being with him and hopes that their relationship grows stronger.

Circle.

Sam is . . .

      thrifty.   compassionate.   extravagant.   perfect.   attentive.

Check.

Sam would probably enjoy . . .

☐ a garage sale.   ☐ a new French restaurant.

☐ McDonald's.   ☐ an opening-day sale.

Write.

When is it better not to be nice? Explain. _____

_____

_____

_____

What characteristics does Sam have that you would like in a friend? _____

_____

_____

_____

Being New Is No Fun

Today was Taylor's first day in sixth grade at Dukwilma School. Before she went through the front door she knew she wouldn't like the school or students and that no one would like her. She really didn't care because she thinks she can make her parents move back to their old town. There's no way they'll like this place. It's nothing like the town they came from.

When Taylor arrived at Dukwilma she laughed at the small school. Her old one was twice as big and newer too. As she walked down the halls to her classroom, Taylor scoffed at the projects hanging on the walls. The projects they did in her old school were much better.

Finally Taylor reached the sixth-grade classroom. There was only one sixth-grade class, so it was easy to find. Only 20 students were in her class. "Great!" thought Taylor. "How boring." Her other school had two sixth-grade classes with over 30 students in each.

When she opened the door to the classroom, Miss Freed and the students surprised Taylor with a welcoming party. Taylor glared at them. She did not want a party from these strange people. She wouldn't eat any of the cake they offered her, and she refused to drink any of Miss Freed's special punch. The party was a disaster. Taylor was unresponsive to the friendly gestures made by the sixth graders, and they, in turn, found themselves not wanting to get to know this unfriendly stranger.

Check.

Taylor is . . .

☐ open-minded.   ☐ insecure.   ☐ pessimistic.

☐ unresponsive to others.   ☐ rude.

Underline.

Taylor constantly . . .

compared Dukwilma to her other school.   made herself approachable to others.

cut down Dukwilma.   had a positive outlook on her situation.

Write.

List some reasons why you think Taylor acted this way.

_____

_____

What are some other things the students could do to help Taylor feel at home? _____

_____

_____

•SOMETHING EXTRA•

Write how you would act if you were in Taylor's situation.

Look Out, It's Gonna Blow!

Kim's dad, Mr. Kare, just got back from Hawaii. While there, he visited Mauna Loa, the world's largest volcano. Miss Freed asked Kim's dad to come in to talk about volcanoes. He happily agreed.

Miss Freed's students already knew that a volcano is an opening in the earth's surface through which lava, hot gases, and rock fragments erupt. Mr. Kare told them that this kind of opening occurs when melted rock, called magma, blasts through the surface from deep within the earth. The students thought this was pretty cool.

Mr. Kare explained that volcanic eruptions are spectacular sights. He said sometimes fiery clouds rise over the volcanic mountain and rivers of hot lava flow down its sides. He said that at other times, red-hot ash and cinders shoot out of the mountaintop and large chunks of hot rock blast high into the air. Mr. Kare also told them that some eruptions are so violent that they blow the mountain apart.

Of course all the students wanted to know why a volcano erupts. Kim helped answer that question. She said that when rock melts inside the earth, it produces a lot of gas which then mixes with the magma. Then she explained that the gas-filled magma slowly rises toward the earth's surface since it is lighter than the solid rock around it. As the magma rises, gaps in the surrounding rock melt. Kim told them that as more magma rises, it forms a large chamber as close as two miles to the surface. The volcanic materials erupt from this magma chamber. Kim's friends were impressed by the presentation, and they all decided they would like to see a volcano.

Check.

The following help cause a volcano to erupt:

☐ A chamber is formed.   ☐ Gas and magma mix.

☐ Gas mixes with solid rock.   ☐ Gas-filled magma rises toward the surface.

Underline.

When a volcano erupts, some of the effects include . . .

huge, fiery clouds.   rivers of hot lava.   the creation of a magma chamber.   shooting hot ash.

Write.

List the causes of a volcanic eruption. _____

_____

_____

List the effects of a volcanic eruption. _____

_____

Name _____

Earthquakes

Suddenly one day while Miss Freed's sixth graders were taking a spelling test, the lights flickered, chalk dropped off the chalkboard, and books fell off the shelves. No one knew what was happening. Then, just as suddenly as the strange occurrence started, it stopped. Dukwilma had experienced a small earthquake. Of course Miss Freed found this to be the perfect time to study earthquakes.

Miss Freed told her students that earthquakes can be explained according to the plate tectonics theory. In this theory, the Earth's surface consists of about 30 rigid plates that move slowly past one another. This motion causes rocks at the plates' edges to be strained and stressed. When the force is too great, the rocks break and shift and an earthquake occurs. Miss Freed also said that most of the breaks, or faults, lie beneath the surface. Others, however, such as the San Andreas Fault in California, are visible.

Jack and Cassie pointed out the damage that can occur in an earthquake. Why, just with the little one they had, all the chalk was broken and books had to be reshelved. Maria quickly reminded them of the recent earthquake in California. Major highways crumbled, houses fell, many fires started, and myriads of other problems occurred. Lee also pointed out that earthquakes can damage water pipes, electric lines, and gas mains. Miss Freed and her students considered themselves very lucky after their study of the damage earthquakes can cause.

Match.

cause of earthquake   Thirty rigid plates move slowly past one another.

effect of earthquake   Rocks break and shift.

                                       Fires start, buildings crumble, debris falls.

                                       Rocks at plates' edges are strained and stressed.

Check.

Some effects earthquakes can have include:

☐ emotional trauma   ☐ falling bricks   ☐ rocks straining

☐ loss of life   ☐ physical injury   ☐ plates sliding

Write.

In your own words, write what causes an earthquake. _____

_____

_____

•SOMETHING EXTRA•

Do you know what to do during an earthquake? Make a list of things to do if one occurs.

Celebrate 6th Graders

What a great day it's going to be! It's *Celebrate Sixth Grade Day* at Dukwilma. The sixth graders may wear whatever they choose and play games and eat treats all day! Miss Freed's students earned this special day by winning a schoolwide competition held between the classes to see who could collect the most recyclable materials. The sixth graders spent three weekends working hard to win.

Since the students collected over five hundred aluminum cans, they earned $75 when they turned them in to the city. As a "thank you," the city offered to buy pizza for the sixth graders. They all agreed to have the pizza on their special day.

As the sixth graders began arriving at school, they were disgusted to see trash littered all over the playground. Who could have done such a thing? As they began cleaning the schoolyard, they spied a group of seventh graders laughing at them. The seventh graders had been close to winning the special day when the sixth graders pulled ahead at the last moment. So the seventh graders, out of jealousy, trashed the playground. When Mrs. Farrell, the principal, learned of the seventh-graders nasty trick, she had them pick up the rest of the litter and act as servants of the sixth graders for the day. The sixth graders had the best day ever.

Match.

Cause	Effect
7th graders spread trash around the playground.	7th graders became servants.
6th graders turned in over 500 cans.	6th graders received free pizza.
6th graders collected the most recyclable materials.	6th graders got a special day.
City was pleased with 6th graders work.	6th graders earned $75.

Underline.

The sixth graders were probably _____ when they saw the trash all over school.

sickened   surprised   elated   ostentatious   malicious

Write.

List as many causes and resulting effects as you can from the story. _____

_____

_____

_____

•SOMETHING EXTRA•

Summarize the story in three sentences.

_____

What's the Difference?

One day, David and Donald were discussing alligators. David insisted that alligators and crocodiles were the same animal but that people called them by different names. Donald insisted, however, that the two animals were entirely different reptiles. Kim walked up just in time to save the boys from further squabbling. Kim, who lived in Florida for ten years, could settle this one.

She told David that yes, alligators and crocodiles were indeed separate reptiles. She told them that although they are similar looking and are both called crocodilians, they are very different. Both have a long, low, cigar-shaped body, short legs, and a long, powerful tail to help them swim, but most crocodiles have a pointed snout instead of a round one like the alligator's. She also pointed out that while both have tough hides, long snouts, and sharp teeth to grasp their prey, the crocodile is only about two-thirds as heavy as an American alligator of the same length and can therefore move much more quickly. David and Donald were impressed with Kim's knowledge.

Kim also told the boys of another way to tell the two reptiles apart. She said that both have an extra long lower fourth tooth. This tooth fits into a pit in the alligator's upper jaw, while in the crocodile, it fits into a groove in the side of the upper jaw and shows when the crocodile's mouth is closed. David and Donald thanked Kim for the information, looked at each other sheepishly, and walked away laughing.

Match.

crocodile   fourth tooth shows when mouth is shut

                            fourth tooth is in a pocket in upper jaw

alligator   round snout

                            called crocodilian

                            pointed snout

Write.
Write three ways alligators and crocodiles are alike and three ways they are different.

1. _____   1. _____
2. _____   2. _____
3. _____   3. _____

Underline.
The crocodile . . .

    has a long snout.   is called a crocodilian.   is fast.

    has long, low legs.   has a round snout.   is a reptile.

•SOMETHING EXTRA•
Name two other animals that are sometimes thought to be the same.

An Exciting Exchange

Miss Freed's best friend from college visited her class today. All the sixth graders were excited about the visit because the friend, Mrs. Cho, lives in Peking, China. Miss Freed thought Mrs. Cho's visit would be a great way for her students to learn about China. She had them prepare questions.

Arnold surprised everyone when he told Mrs. Cho that the United States is the fourth largest country in the world in area and the third largest in population. He then wanted to know about the size of China. Mrs. Cho explained that China, too, is a big country. She told the class that it is the world's largest country in population and the third largest in area. The class was impressed.

Maria wanted to know about Chinese families. Mrs. Cho stated that almost all adults in China have a job. She said that many Chinese children go to nursery school or stay with a grandparent so their mothers can work. She also added that, as in much of the United States, many young husbands share in the duties of shopping, cleaning, cooking, and caring for the kids.

Kim asked Mrs. Cho if she ate anything other than rice. Mrs. Cho laughed. She told the students that she, like the Chinese, eats a lot of grain, especially rice. However, they also enjoy a variety of vegetables and fruit. Meat, she explained, does not play as big a role in the Chinese diet as it does in the American diet. And, Mrs. Cho told them that tea continues to be the favorite beverage. Miss Freed's students said that they were sure that soda pop is the favorite U.S. drink. The students had a great time talking with Mrs. Cho and were glad she came.

Write.

List the differences Arnold learned about between China and the United States when he asked Mrs. Cho a question. _____

_____

_____

Match.

China   Fourth largest country in area.

                               People generally eat a lot of meat.

United States   People love tea.

                               Third largest country in area.

Underline.

Meat is not _____ part of the Chinese diet.

an extensive   a projected   an atrocious   a petty

•SOMETHING EXTRA•

Compare the United States to another country. Share your findings with the class.

Civilization Similarities

For the past month, the sixth graders at Dukwilma have been studying ancient civilizations. So far, they have learned about the ancient Greeks and Romans. The students were surprised at how interesting both civilizations were. They decided to teach the fifth graders about the ancient civilizations. Below are some of the things they told them.

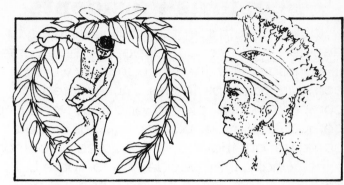

Although both civilizations began over two thousand years ago, Greek civilization is older. It began around 2000 B.C. Legend says Roman civilization began in 753 B.C. Ancient Greece is known as the birthplace of Western civilization. The early Greeks made many advancements in government, science, philosophy, and the arts that influence our lives today.

Ancient Romans also had an enormous impact on the development of Western civilization. It was the Roman principles of justice and the Roman political system which shaped the formation of governments in the United States. Their roads, bridges, and aqueducts have also had an impact on the way many of these things are built in our country today.

In ancient Greece, civilization developed chiefly in small city-states. These consisted of a city or town and the surrounding villages and farmland. Ancient Rome, however, imposed central authority on big areas while still keeping local government. Roman rule gradually spread over all the lands bordering the Mediterranean Sea.

The fifth graders wanted the sixth graders to tell them more about the ancient civilizations of Greece and Rome. But the sixth graders stopped and told them they would have to wait to find out more on their own.

Write.
List the similarities and differences between ancient Greece and Rome.

Similarities	Differences
1. _____	1. _____
2. _____	2. _____
3. _____	3. _____

Match.

Ancient Greece   applied central authority on large areas.

Ancient Rome   built impressive aqueducts and bridges.

                                  developed in city-states.

                                  had an impact on the U.S.

Circle.

Ancient Rome and Greece were _____ in helping make the U.S. what it is today.

preemptive   possessive   influential   irrevocable

•SOMETHING EXTRA•
What is the oldest civilization? Where did it begin?

People as Presidents

Jack and Beth spent several hours trying to decide which two famous people they wanted to compare. First, they thought they would compare famous athletes. Jack wanted to compare football players, and Beth wanted to compare volleyball players. Famous authors came up, but they could not agree on authors either. Finally, they decided to compare U.S. Presidents. They each picked a number be-tween one and 42. They chose ten and 15. It was decided. They would compare John Tyler, our tenth President, and James Buchanan, our fifteenth.

Jack and Beth were surprised to learn how similar Tyler and Buchanan were. For instance, both went to college and practiced law. They both ran successfully for seats in the U.S. House of Representatives: Tyler in 1816 and Buchanan four years later. Jack learned that Tyler was elected to the U.S. Senate in 1827 and that Buchanan followed him there seven years later. But he also noted that whereas Buchanan went on to become Secretary of State and minister to Great Britain after serving about ten years in the Senate, Tyler went from the Senate to become Vice-President of the United States under William Henry Harrison. Beth then told Jack that Tyler became President only one month after Harrison's inauguration due to Harrison's death. Buchanan, Beth noted, was elected President.

Beth and Jack went on to learn that three new states entered the Union under Buchanan and that under Tyler, China opened its ports to American trade and Florida joined the Union.

When they were done researching for their comparison, Jack and Beth were surprised at the amount of information they had gathered. Now came the hard part of putting it all together!

Fill in.
The following apply to **a.** Tyler, or **b.** Buchanan. Put the appropriate letter in the box.

☐ became President when Harrison died   ☐ elected President

☐ Secretary of State   ☐ Vice-President

☐ three new states entered the Union during his presidency   ☐ Florida joined the Union during his presidency

Write.
List similarities and differences between Tyler and Buchanan.

Similarities	Differences
1. _____	1. _____
2. _____	2. _____
3. _____	3. _____
4. _____	4. _____

•SOMETHING EXTRA•
Compare any two famous people of your choice.

Miss Freed's Fascinating Friend

Miss Freed is enthusiastic about her new friend, who is an astronaut. She has enjoyed sharing the information she's acquired about astronauts with her students. They have written it all down, and have even done research on their own to learn more!

Cassie and Maria did a report on "Achievements in Space." It included information on special people such as Russian Yuri A. Gagarin, the first person to travel in space, and Alan B. Shepard, Jr., the first American space traveler. Their report also mentioned Neil A. Armstrong and Edwin E. Aldrin, Jr., the first people to set foot on the moon. Jack and Donald researched how astronauts are selected. They hope someday to become astronauts. The boys learned that two kinds of astronauts are chosen for the various U.S. manned space programs—pilot astronauts and mission specialist astronauts. Jack was upset because a bachelor's degree in engineering, physical science, or math is necessary to qualify as a pilot astronaut. None of these subjects interest Jack very much.

Some of the other topics Miss Freed's students researched included famous astronauts, the training of astronauts, and cosmonauts. They had fun building on the knowledge Miss Freed provided.

Check.

The main idea of the story is . . .

☐ Miss Freed has a new friend who is an astronaut.

☐ An astronaut shared interesting information about astronauts with Miss Freed's class.

☐ Miss Freed stimulated her students' interest in astronauts.

☐ Astronauts are exciting and fascinating.

Underline.

Miss Freed is _____ about her new friend, the astronaut.

excited   embarrassed   charmed   appalled   flourished

Write.

Summarize the story in three sentences. _____

_____

_____

•SOMETHING EXTRA•

Write a story about a pretend trip you took to the moon.

Family Tree Time

Every year, the sixth graders at Dukwilma School research their family trees. Miss Freed finished her family tree years ago. She told the class that she is related to fierce pirates who once roamed the seas. She enjoyed the students' reactions when they found out about their unusual and interesting ancestors.

This year, Lee was the first to discover that he is related to an interesting personality. In old family records he found at the library, Lee was able to trace his roots back to the 1700s. He learned that his great-great-great-great-uncle was John Adams, our second President of the United States. Lee was enthralled to learn that not only was one of his ancestors a president but that he also signed the Declaration of Independence! Lee even attributed his shortness and ruddy complexion to this historic uncle.

Arnold also made an exciting discovery when he learned that Benedict Arnold is his cousin on his great-great-great-grandmother's side. He was sure that it was he who he was named after and seemed proud to be related to this famous U.S. traitor. Do you know who your ancestors are?

Circle.
The main idea of the story is . . .

All the sixth graders at Dukwilma researched a family tree.

Researching a family tree is both fun and interesting for Miss Freed and her students.

Miss Freed loves to hear about her students' ancestors and relatives.

Everyone is related to at least one famous person.

Check.
Miss Freed's students could possibly learn the following information from researching their family trees:

☐ medical facts ☐ attributes ☐ history ☐ modern economics ☐ geography

Write.
Which person would you most like to be related to: John Adams or Benedict Arnold? Why?

•SOMETHING EXTRA•
Research your own family tree. Share any important discoveries with the class.

Brainy Information

Maria's father is a brain surgeon. He knows most of what there is to know about this important organ of the central nervous system. One day he even showed Maria a real human brain and explained its functions. To share with her classmates what she learned, Maria's father gave her an artificial brain to take to school.

Jackie would like to be a doctor someday, so she studies the human body. She pointed out the three parts of the brain for Maria—the cerebrum, the cerebellum, and the brain stem. Then Maria went on to explain the functions of these three parts.

Maria explained that the cerebrum analyzes, processes, and stores information and so makes possible our higher mental abilities, such as thinking, speaking, and remembering. She said that the cerebellum is the part most responsible for balance, posture, and physical coordination. The brain stem, she explained, links the cerebrum with the spinal cord. The bottom part of the brain stem, the medulla, has nerve centers that control breathing, heartbeat, and other vital body processes. At the upper end of the brain stem are the thalamus and hypothalamus. She explained that the thalamus receives nerve impulses from various parts of the body and routes them to the cerebral cortex. It also relays impulses from one part of the brain to the other. The hypothalamus regulates body temperature and hunger.

Miss Freed was impressed with Maria's knowledge of the brain and gave her five extra credit points.

Underline.

The main idea of the story is . . .

Maria shared her knowledge of the brain with her classmates.

The brain has three parts—the cerebrum, the cerebellum, and the brain stem.

If you want to be a doctor, you need to study the human body.

Maria learned important information about the brain from her father.

Match.

brain stem	responsible for physical coordination
cerebrum	helps sort messages and transfers them to the correct part of the brain
cerebellum	controls thinking and decision-making processes

Write.

List some activities you do daily or weekly and note which part of the brain is responsible for each.

_____

_____

_____

Nutty Nutrition

David's mom is a nutritionist. She often tells him to eat right. David is familiar with the food group pyramid and knows he needs to eat plenty of foods from the bottom of the pyramid and very few from the top. But sometimes he doesn't have time to or doesn't feel like eating right. All that needs to change now. David wants to join the basketball team and has to get in shape.

Before, if David got up late, he would grab a candy bar before pedaling off to school with Jack. If he wanted more time to play at lunch, David simply gulped down a cookie. After school, David would grab chips before he practiced basketball. He usually made it home in time for a good dinner – thank goodness! He was always hungry by dinnertime and usually very grouchy.

David's mom says she'll help him change his eating habits. She has him take an inventory of the foods he has been eating. She and David are surprised at the amount of junk he consumes every day. No wonder he is too tired to run and often feels dizzy and out of breath at practice.

David's mom says, "You are what you eat." She explains the importance of the correct amount of carbohydrates (breads, cereals, corn, potatoes), fats (butter, oil), proteins (cheese, eggs, fish, meat, beans), minerals (calcium, magnesium, phosphorous), and vitamins in a diet. These nutrients help us grow. David knows he has to start eating right, so the two sit down and make a daily menu he intends to follow. He also takes in the menu to share with his friends at Dukwilma. They need to eat better, too!

Write.

The main idea of the story is _____

Check.

The following nutrients are essential in a good diet:

☐ fats   ☐ starches   ☐ hemoglobin   ☐ minerals   ☐ saturations

☐ sugars   ☐ carbohydrates   ☐ proteins   ☐ solvents   ☐ vitamins

Match.

fats	calcium, magnesium, phosphorous
proteins	A, B1, B12, C, D, E
carbohydrates	bread, cereal, corn, potatoes
vitamins	butter, oil, shortening
minerals	beans, eggs, cheese, meat, fish

•SOMETHING EXTRA•

Keep track of what you eat for three days. If necessary, create a healthy menu for yourself.

Niagara Falls — Here We Come!

Miss Freed's class is very lucky. The students entered an essay contest on why their class should visit Niagara Falls — and they won! The students and Miss Freed will fly to New York from Dukwilma and spend two nights and three days. Everyone is thrilled.

Before they leave, Miss Freed wants to be sure her students know everything they can about the falls so they will fully enjoy and appreciate the trip. She asks all of them to do some research on the falls. Jack and Jackie find that Niagara Falls is actually two waterfalls, the Horseshoe Falls and the American Falls. Maria reveals that Horseshoe Falls is on the Canadian side.

Lee surprises everyone when he tells them that each fall is about as high as 12 Dukwilma School buildings stacked together — Horseshoe Falls is 167 feet high and American Falls is 176 feet high.

Miss Freed wants her students to notice the different kinds of stone in and around the falls. She tells them that about 80 feet of a hard rock called dolomite forms the top layer and covers softer layers of limestone, sandstone, and shale.

Kim concludes by telling everyone that Niagara Falls was probably formed about 12,000 years ago and that large numbers of tourists first began visiting it during the 1800s. Everyone is eager and ready to go!

Check.

The main idea of the story is . . .

☐ Miss Freed's class is lucky to get to visit Niagara Falls.

☐ Niagara Falls consists of two waterfalls, the Horseshoe Falls and the American Falls.

☐ Jack and Jackie knew more about the falls than anyone else.

☐ Miss Freed's class is excited to learn about and visit Niagara Falls.

Write.

Some things you learned about Niagara Falls from the story are . . . _____

_____

_____

Underline.

Miss Freed tried to _____ her class for the trip so that they would _____ it.

help/enjoy   excite/share   prepare/appreciate   warn/enjoy

•SOMETHING EXTRA•

Write about a natural phenomenon you would like to or have already visited. Share your report with the class.

Flamingo Facts

Cassie and Maria both have pen pals in foreign countries. They love receiving letters from their pen pals because they learn lots of fascinating information about their friends and the countries in which they live. Cassie's pen pal is from Japan. Maria's pen pal, Juanita, lives in Chile.

Just yesterday, Maria received a rather perplexing letter from her Chilean pen pal. Juanita is concerned about the dwindling numbers of flamingos in her country. About 150,000 flamingos live in lakes within a 120,000-square-mile slice of Peru, Chile, Bolivia, and Argentina. But Chile's original population of 75,000 flamingos has declined to 7,000 in four years. No one knows why. Some believe the flamingos migrated to Bolivia. However, Juanita has also heard that some local people steal flamingo eggs to sell as food. This upsets her because female flamingos lay only one egg a year which a nesting pair later raise together. Juanita also loves to watch these beautiful pink birds eating in the water where she lives near the Andes Mountains.

Maria shared this information with her class. Miss Freed decided to investigate this troubling matter. She learned that the Chilean Forestry Department has provided rangers to protect at least one flock of flamingos from eggers since 1985. This project is supported by Wildlife Conservation International, part of the New York Zoological Society.

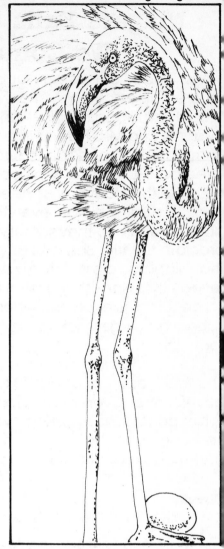

Write.

Maria's pen pal is angry about _____

Match.

disturbing	Chile's flamingo population of 75,000 has declined to 7,000.
exciting	Eggers are stealing flamingo eggs.
perplexing	Maria and Cassie receive letters from pen pals who live in foreign countries.

Check.

Chilean flamingos are . . .

☐ beautiful.   ☐ helpful.   ☐ in trouble.   ☐ disappearing.   ☐ protected.

Write.

Why is Maria's pen pal angered that flamingo eggs are sold as food?

•SOMETHING EXTRA•

Write about an endangered animal in your area.

Lucky Lee

David is envious of Lee. Lee is going on an-other great vacation. This time he and his parents are traveling to Alaska to climb the majestic Mount McKinley, which is the highest peak in the United States. Just last summer, Lee's family went on a safari in Africa. Lee saw herds of elephants, fierce lions, and even a few leopards. David would have loved to travel to Africa.

Lee tells David and some of their other friends that he will be visiting Denali National Park and Preserve. David wants to show Lee that he knows a lot about the park, so he looks up some quick facts. "Oh, yeah," says David. "It covers six million acres. Did you know that that's slightly larger than the state of Massachusetts?" "Sure did," replies Lee. "It's the fourth largest unit within the National Park System. And visitors can usually see a greater variety of animals here than a lot of other places." "More than Africa?" asks David. "Probably," replies Lee. David is green with envy.

David can imagine seeing grizzly bears and moose and then climbing to the very top of the 20,320 foot peak of Mount McKinley. Gosh, he'd probably make it to the top by noon and then climb back down before dinner. What great things he would see and great stories he would tell! One of these days . . .

Write.
Why is David envious of Lee? _____

_____

_____

Check.
Lee is going to do the following on his trip:

☐ hunt elephants, lions, and leopards.

☐ see a variety of animals.

☐ climb Mount McKinley.

☐ visit an eight-million-acre park and preserve.

Circle.

Circle the true statements.

David will be able to climb Mount McKinley in a few hours.

Lee saw elephants and leopards in Africa.

Mount McKinley is 20,320 feet tall.

Denali National Park and Preserve covers six million acres.

•SOMETHING EXTRA•
Find out about the mountains that are closest to your city/town. How high is the highest peak?

What a Whale Shark!

Miss Freed is surprising her class with a field trip to a sealife exhibit. She knows that her students will be excited because the main attraction at the exhibit is a whale shark. Her sixth graders are fascinated by this monstrous but docile creature. They first learned about the whale shark, the largest fish in the world, when they were studying ocean life. It seemed they couldn't get enough information about it.

Beth and Kim gave a great report on the whale shark. They reported that this up-to-50-foot-long fish eats plankton and small schooling fish. Some whale sharks have even let divers grab on to their dorsal fin and go for a ride.

Jack learned that the whale shark may be found in a band around the equator extending roughly 30° north and 35° south. He reported that they seem to prefer surface-water temperatures in the 70s or low 80s.

Always concerned with protecting animals, Cassie pointed out in her research that the whale shark has much more to fear from humans than humans have to fear from it. These gentle animals are harpooned and eaten near India and in Taiwan. The Japanese, however, don't like to kill the whale shark. It supposedly brings good luck and is named after a patron god of the sea. Miss Freed wonders how they managed to get a fish as large as this in the exhibit. The students are going to love this field trip.

Check.

The whale shark is . . .

☐ a fish. ☐ a shark. ☐ gentle. ☐ huge. ☐ the largest fish in the world.

Match.

Match the person(s) to the fact he or she reported.

Kim and Beth   The whale shark has a lot to fear from humans.

Cassie   Whale sharks eat plankton and small fish.

Jack   Whale sharks like warmer waters.

Underline.

The Japanese think the whale shark . . .

should be eaten.   brings good luck.   is dangerous.

Write.

Why does the whale shark have more to fear from humans than humans do from whale sharks?

_____

_____

•SOMETHING EXTRA•

Make up a story about a ride you took on a whale shark.

Mrithi's Misfortune

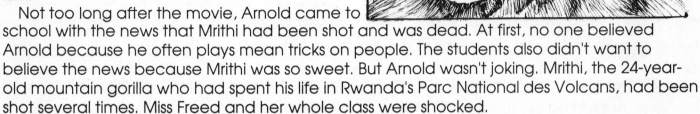

One afternoon before spring break, Miss Freed surprised her sixth graders with the movie *Gorillas in the Mist*. They were very excited because they had been studying wild animals and the dangers they face in our world. The students adored the movie and especially loved Mrithi, a mountain gorilla featured in the film.

Not too long after the movie, Arnold came to school with the news that Mrithi had been shot and was dead. At first, no one believed Arnold because he often plays mean tricks on people. The students also didn't want to believe the news because Mrithi was so sweet. But Arnold wasn't joking. Mrithi, the 24-year-old mountain gorilla who had spent his life in Rwanda's Parc National des Volcans, had been shot several times. Miss Freed and her whole class were shocked.

Mrithi's loss stunned observers, who feared that civil war would bring even more gorilla deaths and loss of habitat to the roughly 600 mountain gorillas remaining in the wild. The director of the park's veterinary center said she believed it was an accident, but she was very worried that it could happen again. It was unclear whether government soldiers or Rwandan rebels killed this leader of a 12-member family. All of Miss Freed's students hope that Ukwacumi, a 12-year-old male gorilla, will keep the surviving members together.

Write.

Why was Miss Freed's class excited to watch *Gorillas in the Mist*?

_____

_____

Check.

Check the items below which pertain to Mrithi.

☐ 22-year-old gorilla   ☐ movie star   ☐ lived in Uganda

☐ leader of a 12-member family   ☐ shot by government soldiers or Rwandan rebels   ☐ lived in Rwanda

Circle.

No one believed Mrithi was really dead because . . .

Arnold said it.   the news was too sad.   he lived in Parc National des Volcans.

Write.

Write down three details found in the story that help make it interesting.

_____

_____

•SOMETHING EXTRA•

Write about a film you enjoyed that relates to something you have studied in class.

Sorting Through a Horrible Mess

Several of the parents of Miss Freed's students served in the Vietnam War. These include Jackie and Beth's fathers as well as Lee's mom. These sixth graders don't know much about this war or why it lasted almost 18 years.

Help Miss Freed's students better understand what went on during this time by sorting

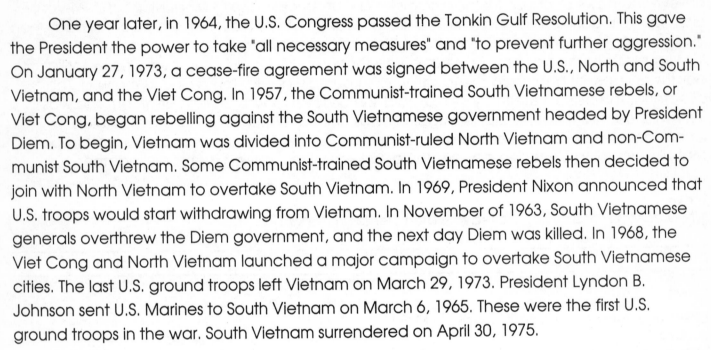

through the information below and organizing it chronologically on the lines provided. **Hint:** If two lines are provided, two sentences should be written.

One year later, in 1964, the U.S. Congress passed the Tonkin Gulf Resolution. This gave the President the power to take "all necessary measures" and "to prevent further aggression." On January 27, 1973, a cease-fire agreement was signed between the U.S., North and South Vietnam, and the Viet Cong. In 1957, the Communist-trained South Vietnamese rebels, or Viet Cong, began rebelling against the South Vietnamese government headed by President Diem. To begin, Vietnam was divided into Communist-ruled North Vietnam and non-Communist South Vietnam. Some Communist-trained South Vietnamese rebels then decided to join with North Vietnam to overtake South Vietnam. In 1969, President Nixon announced that U.S. troops would start withdrawing from Vietnam. In November of 1963, South Vietnamese generals overthrew the Diem government, and the next day Diem was killed. In 1968, the Viet Cong and North Vietnam launched a major campaign to overtake South Vietnamese cities. The last U.S. ground troops left Vietnam on March 29, 1973. President Lyndon B. Johnson sent U.S. Marines to South Vietnam on March 6, 1965. These were the first U.S. ground troops in the war. South Vietnam surrendered on April 30, 1975.

1. _____
   _____
2. _____
3. _____
4. _____
   _____
5. _____
   _____
6. _____
7. _____
8. _____
9. _____
10. _____

Fantastic Philanthropist

The sixth-grade students in Miss Freed's class have decided to become philanthropists. They have agreed to set apart one day each month on which to hold a bake sale or car wash to raise money for a good cause or to help others in need. Miss Freed has been teaching her students about some of the famous philanthropists in our country. One of them is John Davison Rockefeller. To learn about his life, number the boxes below in the correct order. Cut each one apart and glue it to its own page. Illustrate the pages and put them in order. Then you will have a biography of Rockefeller.

In 1882, Rockefeller organized the Standard Oil Trust. At this time, he controlled almost all U.S. oil refining and distribution and much of the world's oil trade.	Rockefeller's Standard Oil Company controlled the flow of all oil products from producer to consumer.
From 1895 to 1897, Rockefeller gradually retired from business. He had already started his vast philanthropic activities.	John Davison Rockefeller was born in 1839 in New York.
By 1910, he had given about $35 million to the University of Chicago. In all, Rockefeller gave away about $520 million during his lifetime. He died in 1937.	In 1890, Rockefeller helped found the University of Chicago.
The trust was dissolved because of the vastness of Rockefeller's holdings and because of public criticism of his methods.	Rockefeller used the profits from the grain house to enter the oil business in about 1862.
When Rockefeller was 14 years old, his family moved to Cleveland where he started work as a clerk in a small produce firm at age 16.	Fifteen years after he had entered the oil business, Rockefeller achieved his goal of making the oil industry orderly and efficient with the Standard Oil Company.
He formed a partnership in a grain commission house after working as a clerk.	About two years later, in 1892, the Ohio Supreme Court dissolved the Standard Oil Trust.

•**SOMETHING EXTRA**•

If you had $520 million dollars to give away, who would you give it to?

Miss Freed's Special Day

Cassie and Kim overheard Miss Freed tell the 7th grade teacher that she was having another birthday. This one was special because she was going to be 40! Wow! Miss Freed is old! Cassie and Kim decided they would tell the rest of the class so they could throw a party for her. After all, how many more birthdays could she have?

So the students got together and planned a special day for Miss Freed. They decided to surprise her with a big cake and a mural of her life.

Help the sixth graders put the information they gathered about Miss Freed from her friends in chronological order. **Note:** Just for fun, pretend it is the year 2000. Then read all of the clues before you begin. This will help you determine the years in which the events occurred. Write the correct years in the spaces provided.

_____ Twenty-eight years before her fortieth birthday, Miss Freed went to summer camp and broke her arm. She was thrown off her horse after it was stung by a bee.

_____ Twenty-nine years after Miss Freed's birth, Sam Spacey saw her and said it was love at first sight.

_____ Miss Freed was born in the back seat of her parents' car during a huge snowstorm.

_____ Miss Freed turns 40! She's over the hill!

_____ Miss Freed got her very first pair of glasses 14 years before she lost her speech at the Governor's Ball.

_____ Twenty years before Miss Freed took her class to the zoo, she asked six boys to go to the Sadie Hawkins Day dance before one accepted. Two of them had the flu, one had to go out of town, one was grounded, and one had to babysit his little brother.

_____ Poor Miss Freed! Twelve years before she won "teacher of the year," Miss Freed was chosen to speak at the Governor's Ball, and she lost her speech! She just stood there and blushed.

_____ Miss Freed won the award of "teacher of the year" at Dukwilma School just eight years after she was hired there.

_____ Seven years after Sam Spacey fell in love with her, Miss Freed took her class on a field trip to the zoo.

_____ Miss Freed was hired as a teacher at Dukwilma School eight years after the Sadie Hawkins dance.

Arnold's Awful Antics

Arnold was up to his dirty tricks again. This time he really did it! Miss Freed was out sick, and the sixth graders had a substitute teacher, Miss Spencer. Poor unsuspecting Miss Spencer asked for a volunteer to write some information on the board for the class to copy. When Arnold raised his hand, Miss Spencer gave him the information. Arnold, as usual, messed things up for everyone. He wrote all the information on the board, but he wrote it out of order. Then, to be even meaner, he tore up the only copy of the information and threw it away!

Help Miss Spencer and the sixth graders write the information below in correct order so that they can learn about the history of baseball.

Also in the late 1800s, 1876 to be exact, the National League was founded. Ty Cobb, Christy Mathewson, Cy Young, and Babe Ruth were just a few of the many early, outstanding base-ball players. About 24 years later, in 1900, the American League was founded. The two major leagues had some great players. Baseball first began in the mid-1800s in the eastern United States. In this modern era, the two major leagues were formed and most baseball rules were the same as today. Current outstanding players are Ozzie Smith and George Brett. Through-out the country, men were playing the game by the late 1800s. It was also in 1900 that the modern era of major league baseball began. Today, baseball is so popular that it is often called our national pastime.

1. _____

2. _____

3. _____

4. _____

5. _____

6. _____

7. _____

8. _____

9. _____

10. _____

Very Interesting Vertebrates

Mr. Fridley, the science teacher, has been teaching Miss Freed's sixth graders about vertebrates. Vertebrates are animals with backbones and a cranium. He asked the students to name as many vertebrates as they could. They came up with frog, chicken, fish, horse, turtle, cow, cat, dog, bird, human, and many others. Mr. Fridley was surprised human was one of their answers, since most people forget that they are vertebrates too.

The students learned about the many characteristics of vertebrates. Mr. Fridley told them that when you say that an animal has a backbone, it does not mean that there is one single bone. Rather, the backbone consists of many bones linked together. He also told them, however, that some vertebrates' backbones, such as the shark, are made of cartilage. Maria said she had read that the backbone is part of the *endoskeleton*—an internal skeleton. Mr. Fridley was excited that Maria knew this. He continued and said that endoskeletons give vertebrates their shape. They also help protect internal organs. For example, the skull protects the brain and the ribs protect the heart and lungs.

Mr. Fridley also said that most vertebrates have two pairs of limbs. Mr. Fridley said that these limbs could be arms, legs, wings, fins, or flippers. He concluded by telling the students that each endoskeleton has bones that connect limbs to the backbone and that a vertebrate's endoskeleton makes it possible for the animal to move. Miss Freed was happy to learn how interested her vertebrates were in other vertebrates

Check.

Vertebrates . . .

☐ have no backbone.

☐ have the same shape.

☐ have an endoskeleton.

☐ include worms, cats, and mice.

☐ include humans, frogs, and dogs.

☐ have a backbone.

Write.

List ten words from the story relating to the word *vertebrate*. _____

_____

List five vertebrates and the two pairs of limbs each one has. _____

_____

Underline.

An invertebrate is probably an animal with . . .

a vertebrate inside.   a backbone inside.   no backbone.

•SOMETHING EXTRA•

What is another way to classify animals?

What's an Invertebrate?

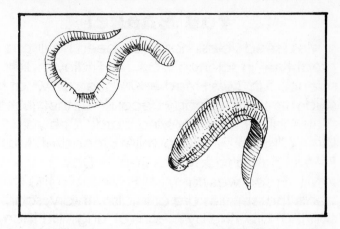

Mr. Fridley arranged for Miss Freed's class to spend a whole morning learning about invertebrates. Miss Freed was very excited for her students.

Off the sixth graders marched to Mr. Fridley's science lab. When they walked in, they were greeted by dozens of pictures of animals hanging from the ceiling, on the walls, and arranged around the room. The students saw pictures of sponges, jellyfish, worms, snails, sea stars, and insects. Mr. Fridley asked the students if they knew what these animals had or didn't have in common. The students thought hard and made lots of guesses. Finally, Kim said, "They don't have a backbone!" She had guessed correctly. Mr. Fridley was proud of her.

Mr. Fridley explained that there are so many invertebrates (more than one million species), and they include so many forms of animals that they have been divided into several major groups. These groups are called phyla. There are nine *phyla*, each with its own characteristics. As an example of a phylum (singular for phyla), Mr. Fridley told them about the phylum *Annelida*, which includes worms with bodies made of segments. The earthworm, sandworm, and leech belong to this group. He then divided the class into eight groups and assigned a phylum for each to research.

Check.

Invertebrates have . . .

☐ a backbone.   ☐ a million different species.   ☐ nothing in common.

☐ major groups called phyla.   ☐ no backbone.   ☐ nine phyla called Annelida.

Write.

List five vertebrates and five invertebrates. What physical differences can you see between these

groups of animals? _____

_____

_____

Underline.

There are _____ numbers of invertebrates.

          multitudinous   myriad   voluminous   scant

Circle.

The singular and plural group names for invertebrates respectively are . . .

   phyla/phylum.   phyla/phylas.   phylum/phylums.   phylum/phyla.

•SOMETHING EXTRA•

List all nine phyla of invertebrates and give an example of each.

You Snake!

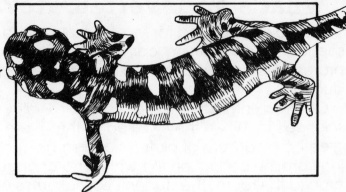

Miss Freed's class has lately been having a great time in science class. Mr. Fridley makes science fun. Miss Freed easily guessed what her students studied today because of their jesting: "You snake!" "You low-lying lizard!" "See ya' later, alligator!" "After awhile, crocodile!" Miss Freed figured today was Reptile Day.

Miss Freed was right. Mr. Fridley told the students that reptiles are animals with dry, scaly skin that breathe by means of lungs. He then assigned each of the sixth graders one of the 6,000 or so kinds of reptiles and asked them to research ten facts about it. Then, each student had to pretend to be that reptile and call out clues about the animal. The students had fun guessing the correct reptiles.

When the game was over, Mr. Fridley asked the students which clues most of the reptiles had in common. The students thought about it and gradually came up with some answers. Donald remembered that they were cold-blooded — that is, their body temperature stays about the same as the temperature of their surroundings. Jack remembered that most reptiles that are active during the day have to keep moving from sunny to shady spots to avoid extremely high or low temperatures. Cassie and Lee both blurted out that reptiles in regions with harsh winters hibernate in the winter. Mr. Fridley was surprised at how much information the students had gathered.

Mr. Fridley then explained that there are four main groups of reptiles — lizards and snakes, turtles, crocodilians, and the tuatara — and that they live in various habitats on every continent except Antarctica. The sixth graders agreed that reptiles are pretty cool.

Match.

Reptiles

live on all continents.

are cold-blooded.

avoid extremely high or low temperatures.

hibernate in winter.

Write.

Explain what cold-blooded means and tell how it affects some reptile behavior. _____

_____

_____

_____

Circle.

Reptiles have many _____ habitats.

          similar   variant   parallel   distinguished

•SOMETHING EXTRA•

Write ten facts about a reptile of your choice.

Realistic or an Impression?

Miss Freed and her sixth grade class are taking a field trip to the art museum. The students aren't very excited because they would rather go to the zoo. Miss Freed knows they will like the museum once they get there.

To prepare her students, Miss Freed has been showing the students paintings by a variety of artists. Some of the paintings were made by such painters as Edouard Manet, Camille Pissarro, Edgar Degas, and Claude Monet. Miss Freed explained that these painters try to show what the eye sees at a glance, rather than what they know in depth about the object or event. This type of art is called *impressionism*.

The other type of art Miss Freed has been exposing her students to is *realism*. Realistic painters attempted to portray life as it is. These artists tried to show what is observed through the senses as accurately as possible. They also strived not to distort life by forcing it to agree with their own desires. Some American realist painters include Reginald Marsh, Thomas Eakins, and Winslow Homer. Miss Freed is anxious to see who paid attention during her explanations of the paintings and plans to give her unsuspecting sixth graders a pop quiz when they arrive at the museum.

Check.
Check the boxes below which relate to realism.

☐ Edgar Degas   ☐ don't distort life   ☐ life portrayed as it is

☐ record what is observed   ☐ show what the eye sees at a glance   ☐ Reginald Marsh

Match.

impressionism

realism

Manet, Monet, Degas, Pissarro

portrays life as it is

does not portray what artist knows in depth

what eye sees at a glance

Underline.
Both types of artists try to _____ life in one way or another.

deplete   berth   impetuate   prognosticate   represent

Write.
If you were a painter, would you be an impressionist or a realist? Why? _____

_____

•SOMETHING EXTRA•
Try your hand at an impressionistic or realistic drawing or painting.

Listen! The Elephants Are Talking

   Miss Freed's class is studying animals that are in danger of becoming extinct. One day, Donald came to class with some interesting information on elephants. Donald read in a magazine that elephants do more than just roar, trumpet, or snort. Donald told his class-mates that they also make sounds that human ears cannot hear.

   Cassie wanted to know how humans would know about these sounds if they couldn't hear them. Donald told Cassie that a biologist named Katherine Payne found out about the sounds in 1984 while she was at a zoo. Donald said that Mrs. Payne felt the air around her throb as she observed the elephants. She thought that this could be low-frequency sounds made by the elephants that she could not hear. Donald pointed out that Mrs. Payne hypoth-esized that the newly discovered elephant sounds could travel over a much greater dis-tance than an elephant's trumpet or roar.

   Jack asked if Mrs. Payne's hypothesis was true. Donald told him that in 1986, Payne went to Africa to test her hypothesis. He said that she wondered if the elephants used the calls to locate each other in the vast African plains and forests. What Mrs. Payne learned was that elephant's foreheads flutter and their ears flap when they make low-frequency calls. These calls seemed to help the elephants find each other. Donald's friends and Miss Freed were impressed with his information.

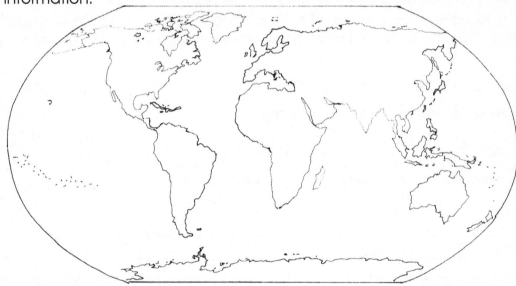

Label.
Mrs. Payne is from North America and traveled to Africa. Label the seven continents above.

Write.
Write the definition of frequency under the title.

Underline.
Underline all of the words with three or more syllables found in the story.

Write.
Mrs. Payne hopes that the elephant's chances of survival will increase. Next to the continents, list some reasons why you think elephants are in danger of becoming extinct.

•SOMETHING EXTRA•
Find out about another animal that is in danger of becoming extinct. What can you do to help it?

Mesopotamia

Miss Freed's sixth graders enjoyed learning about ancient Greece and Rome so much that she decided to teach them about Mesopotamia. She asked what they thought *Mesopotamia* was. Lee thought it sounded like a fancy soup. Jack thought it was a deep, dark hole out in space. Maria and Kim thought it was a foreign word. The rest of the students just wanted Miss Freed to hurry and tell them what it was.

Miss Freed explained that Mesopotamia was the region where the world's first civilization developed. She told them that the word means "between rivers." The heart of Mesopotamia was between the Tigris and Euphrates rivers. Today, parts of the countries of Syria, Turkey, and Iraq are located where Mesopotamia once thrived.

Northern Mesopotamia had a mild climate and received enough rain to enable crops to grow on parts of it. Southern Mesopotamia, often flooded by the Tigris and Euphrates rivers, provided rich farmland for its inhabitants. However, because of the long, hot summers, irrigation was necessary for agriculture.

In about 3500 B.C. new settlers arrived in a part of this region that became known as *Sumer*. The Sumerians, as they were called, built the world's first cities and developed the first civilization. They also invented the world's first system of writing called *cuneiform*.

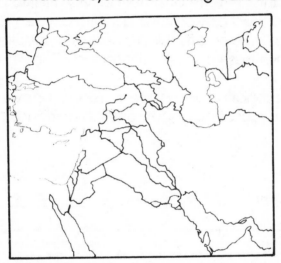

Label.
1. The Tigris River is east of the Euphrates River. Label the rivers.
2. Turkey is north of Syria and Iraq. Iraq is southeast of Syria. Label Turkey, Syria, and Iraq.

Write.
Irrigation began in Mesopotamia in about 5000 B.C. Under the title, write how many years ago this occurred.

Underline.
Underline all of the adjectives on the page.

Write.
On another paper, write why you think civilizations first developed in this area, rather than in a different part of the world.

•SOMETHING EXTRA•
If you could take three things back in time to the first civilization, what you would take and why?

Plant Fun

Miss Freed's sixth graders are excited! They are the first class in Dukwilma to visit the new *Great Green Things Museum*. Lee's dad's company did some work on the museum. As a favor to him, his son's class is first to visit the museum.

The students think the museum is awesome. It's filled with some incredible plants, including some that eat insects! As they tour the museum, a guide explains photosynthesis. Most of the students have already studied photosynthesis, but it seems more real and understandable now that they are surrounded by exotic plants.

The guide explains that photosynthesis is the food-making process of green plants. This is the chief function of leaves. In this process, green plants use energy from light to combine carbon dioxide and water to make food. All our food comes from this important activity.

She further explains that plants perform another activity vital to our existence. They give off oxygen. We, in turn, "burn" the food by combining it with oxygen to release energy. Oxygen is used up and carbon dioxide is given off. This process of respiration is the reverse of photosynthesis. The cycle of photosynthesis and respiration maintains the Earth's natural balance of carbon dioxide and oxygen.

As the guide finishes her explanation, the students feel a renewed appreciation of plants. They tour the remainder of the museum, eager to tell their friends about what they saw and learned.

Write.

1. Write about the importance of oxygen to living things. _____

_____

_____

2. What do you think would happen if all the plants in the world began to die? _____

_____

_____

Figure.
There are about 350,000 varieties of plants. About half of these are flowering. Using these figures, make up a math word problem and exchange it with a friend.

Draw.
Draw a picture depicting photosynthesis. Use an encyclopedia, if necessary.

•SOMETHING EXTRA•
What is your favorite plant. Why?

What a Slithering Mess!

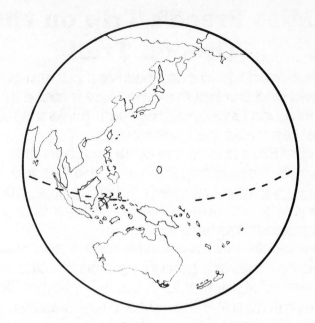

Miss Freed is upset. She and her friend Alice were planning to go to Guam, an island in the Pacific Ocean, for vacation next week. Miss Freed has decided she's not going. She just read that Guam has been overrun by nocturnal brown tree snakes.

Alice tells Miss Freed to relax. She says the snakes will probably disappear soon. But Miss Freed says this isn't so. She says that it is believed that the uninvited guests arrived in Guam as shipboard stowaways after World War II. She also tells Alice that these up-to-ten feet long snakes are mean and slightly poisonous. Alice listens attentively when Miss Freed tells her that the snake has no natural enemies. Alice realizes that if the snake has no enemies, then nothing is killing it. She begins to think she doesn't want to go to Guam either. She's not crazy about snakes.

Miss Freed goes on to tell her that millions of these snakes have decimated Guam wildlife and crawled into homes. That's enough for Alice. Hawaii sounds inviting now. Why didn't they plan to go there in the first place?

The last straw for Alice comes when Miss Freed says that in at least one area of Guam, the density of the snakes has reached about 30,000 per square mile! Alice is definitely not going to Guam. She figures that the approximate 130,000 Guamanians must be terribly outnumbered on their 209-square-mile island. She is not going to join them. Hawaii here they come!

Label.
1. Asia is northwest of Guam, and Australia is southwest of it. Label these on the map.
2. Label the Pacific Ocean.

Write.
Write what you would do to deal with these snakes under the title.

Create.
Create a math word problem using any facts found on this page.

Circle.
Circle the word on this page that means "active at night."

Write.
If you could be a stowaway on a ship, where would you go and why? _____

•SOMETHING EXTRA•
The brown tree snakes have wiped out nine of twelve bird species and subspecies on Guam. Write about the effect this could have on the environment.

Miss Freed's Trip on the Oregon Trail

Jack and Maria can't believe it but Kim can. David and Donald think she'll never make it. Arnold can't stop laughing. Beth thinks she'll do fine. Lee thinks she'll back out.

Miss Freed and all the other teachers at Dukwilma are hitting the trail — the Oregon Trail. They will endure 75 miles of choking dust, punishing winds, and freezing nights just to sharpen their geography skills.

Arnold still laughs when he remembers Miss Freed on the sixth-grade camping trip. She went to the main lodge every day to take a shower, curl her hair, and apply make-up. David and Donald also remember her piercing scream when she thought she saw a snake, which turned out to be a stick.

Miss Freed and the teachers will map out their journey and keep daily logs of soil types, vegetation, and weather. They must be prepared to deal with all the situations this unforgiving terrain may present, just as the 350,000 settlers who crossed the trail during the mid-1800s had to. They are told to bring warm clothing for night since it may get down to 25°. They might also have to push the wagons out of the bogs. And they have been told to forget about riding in the wagons because the trail is so bumpy that they'll want to walk. Miss Freed always seems to be cold, even on the warmest days. And she isn't the rugged outdoors type. The sixth graders can't imagine why their teacher would want to do anything like this.

Check.
Based on Miss Freed's past experiences, she will probably . . .

☐ have a great time.   ☐ get cold.   ☐ help push wagons.

☐ be a mess on the trip. ☐ be a big help.   ☐ be frightened.

Underline.
Miss Freed would probably be more likely to enjoy . . .

a fishing trip.   a week at a resort.   a safari.   a weekend at a spa.

Circle.
You probably wouldn't see Miss Freed . . .

skiing.   hunting.   at a beauty parlor.   rafting.

Write.
What types of activities do you think Miss Freed might enjoy? _____

_____

•SOMETHING EXTRA•
Write what someone would not be likely to see you doing.

_____

The Duks vs. the Dodgers

The sixth graders at Dukwilma School are practicing hard for the big softball game with the sixth graders at Dailey School. The Duks must beat the Dailey Dodgers this year. The Dodgers won last year's game, and it was the worst experience! The losers served the winners pizza and soda pop at a pizza party. This year, the losers will serve lunch to the winners in the losers' school cafeteria — where everyone will see them. The Duks have to win!

Cassie and David, the Duks' team captains, think they have a good chance of winning this year. Jackie, Jack, and Donald can really pound the balls far. They're always hitting home runs. And with Lee pitching and Arnold catching, the Dodgers may never even get a hit. But if they do, Maria, Kim, and Beth will be ready to catch the balls. They're awesome.

The day of the big game arrives. The Dodgers look big and tough. The game begins. The Dodgers get two runs in the first inning. The Duks have to get going. They score three runs! The Dodgers score two more runs in the second and in the third innings. The Duks follow with the same — two runs per inning. The game continues and by the seventh inning the Dodgers are ahead by one. The Duks have one last chance to win. The Duks score and the game's tied. On they go to another inning.

Check.

The Duks were probably playing well because . . .

☐ they really wanted to win.

☐ the Dodgers are rotten players.

☐ they are scared of the Dodgers.

☐ the Duks have great players on their team.

Underline.

Because of the team's well-rounded _____ , the odds of winning the game were in their favor.

alchemy   solicitude   aptness   gesticulations   freehandedness

Write.

How do you think the losing team felt when they served the winning team lunch in their cafeteria?

_____

_____

_____

•SOMETHING EXTRA•

Write about a time your team won an important game.

Fear of the Flood

The whole town of Dukwilma is nervous. There has been so much rain lately that the people are afraid their town will be flooded. Dukwilma hasn't flooded since 1972 when there was so much rain that Dukwilma Creek looked like a river and appeared to flow backwards! This was a sad time because many people's homes and businesses were destroyed by all the water. Those businesses that were spared were shut down for several weeks. Dukwilma was at a virtual standstill. Now there's a chance that this might happen again.

Miss Freed's class decides to study floods to learn how damaging they could be to Dukwilma. Since Dukwilma is located on a river, the sixth graders are mainly concerned with river floods. They find that the common causes of river floods include too much rain and the sudden melting of snow or ice. Under these conditions, the sixth graders read, rivers may receive more than ten times as much water as their beds can hold. The students know that the river on which Dukwilma is situated is already approaching its capacity, and more rain is on its way. Thank goodness for the levee built after the 1972 flood. They hope it will hold the water back. Miss Freed's students are anxious to hear the weather forecast after lunch.

When the forecast does come on, it is as the students have feared. It is predicted that Dukwilma will receive six more inches in the next two days. That's more rain than the town usually gets in three months during this time of year. The students, like everyone else, are very concerned.

Underline.

If Dukwilma gets more rain, the following things could happen.

The levee could break.　　　The school could float away.　　　The students could go boating.

The town could flood.　　　Homes could be lost.　　　Businesses could be lost.

Check.

The effects of the rain could be devastating because . . .

☐ crops could be destroyed.　　☐ businesses could be ruined.　　☐ the town could shut down.

☐ the ground would be wet.　　☐ people won't be able to use the river for fun.

Write.

If your house were in danger of being flooded and you had to evacuate, what would you do?

_____

_____

_____

•SOMETHING EXTRA•

If your house were in danger of being flooded and you could take only three things with you, what would you take and why?

Cassie's Dilemma

For a month, Cassie has been looking forward to her grandparents coming to town. She doesn't care that it's only for one night and a Friday night at that! Cassie usually spends Friday night at Kim or Beth's, but she'll gladly stay home to see her grandparents — especially since her grandfather has been diagnosed with diabetes. Cassie wants to see for herself if her grandpa is doing as well as everyone says.

When Cassie first learned her grandpa had diabetes, she was very upset. She didn't even know what diabetes was. When she researched the disease, she found that the kind of diabetes her grandfather has is *diabetes mellitus*. In this disease, the body cannot use glucose normally and sugar builds up in the blood. Many diabetic patients must take insulin to enable the body to use and store sugar properly. Others are luckier and have a milder form of diabetes and do not need insulin. Cassie's grandfather is one of the lucky ones. Cassie wondered if her grandfather had experienced some of the symptoms of diabetes, which include great thirst, hunger, loss of weight and strength, and excessive urination. He must have or else how would he have known something was wrong?

Three days before her grandparents are scheduled to arrive, Dukwilma School wins the big spelling bee against other area schools. This means Dukwilma's spelling champs will be taking a three-hour trip to Chicago on Friday for a state-wide spelling bee. Cassie is crushed. She is the best speller at her school. If she doesn't go, her school might lose. If she does go, she won't be able to see her grandparents. What will she do?

Check.

Cassie might stay home to see her grandparents because . . .

☐ they'll be there on Friday night.

☐ they'll only be there one night.

☐ her grandpa has diabetes mellitus.

☐ she has been worried about her grandpa.

Circle.

Cassie might go to the spelling bee because . . .

she is the best speller.

her school needs her.

they're going to the state-wide competition.

the spelling bee is in Chicago.

Write.

What do you think Cassie will do? Why? _____

_____

What would you do? Why? _____

_____

•SOMETHING EXTRA•

Write about a big decision you once had to make.

Will Kim Go On?

Miss Freed must make a tough decision. She is preparing report cards for her sixth-grade students. She will miss them when they go on to seventh grade, but she is happy about their progress. The problem is that one of the students might not be promoted. Kim has had a difficult year. Her grades aren't good enough for Miss Freed to pass her. This saddens Miss Freed because if Kim doesn't pass, not only will she not be able to move on, but all of her friends will be leaving her behind. Miss Freed doesn't know what to do since the situation really is not Kim's fault.

Kim was sick with pneumonia for the first three months of school. Her mom came and picked up her books and all of her assignments, but Kim was too sick to care about school. She was in the hospital for three weeks and in bed at home the rest of the time. When Kim recovered, Kim's mom insisted she could catch up. She hired tutors for Kim and did everything possible to help Kim keep up, but Kim was behind right from the start. No matter how hard she tried, Kim couldn't catch up. She had lost too much ground at the beginning. Miss Freed often felt sorry for Kim when she heard the other students making plans for the weekend. Kim would sit there quietly because she knew she'd be studying.

Kim's mom promises that Kim will make up the work over the summer if Miss Freed graduates her. Miss Freed knows Kim is trying and has been improving, but she still isn't sure what to do.

Underline.

Miss Freed is very _____ about Kim's situation.

    pessimistic   enshrouded   literal   vindictive   anxious

Circle.

Kim probably feels _____ about her situation.

    dismal   optimistic   elated   disquieted   distressed

Check.

If Miss Freed passes Kim, then . . .

☐ Kim might stay behind in school work.   ☐ Kim won't need any more tutors.

☐ Kim will definitely catch up.   ☐ Kim will be under a lot of pressure.

☐ Kim's mom will be happy.

Write.

What would you want to do if you were in Kim's shoes? _____

•SOMETHING EXTRA•

What are some new things that might happen in seventh grade?

I Do, or I Don't?

Sam Spacey asked Miss Freed to marry him! The sixth graders are all so excited. He asked her at Dukwilma Day in front of the whole school! The two were running a one-legged race together and were almost at the finish line when Sam tripped and they both fell. While they struggled to get up, Sam pulled a ring out of his pocket and in front of everyone asked Miss Freed to marry him. All the kids cheered as Sam put the ring on Miss Freed's finger. She stood there looking shocked.

The next day, Cassie, Maria, and Beth asked Miss Freed when the wedding would be. Miss Freed blushed and said very quietly to the girls that she hadn't made up her mind yet. The girls assumed she hadn't made up her mind about the date. However, Miss Freed went on to tell them that she and Mr. Spacey had a lot to talk about before she could say yes. The three girls were amazed. What did they have to talk about? All they had to do was get married. Miss Freed explained that there were many things they had to consider before getting married. For instance, they both own houses, so whose would they live in? Plus, Sam lives in Dailey and she lives in Dukwilma, so they also had to decide in which town to live. Miss Freed has a cat, and Sam is allergic to cats. What would happen to Hairy? And, Miss Freed wants at least two children, but Sam isn't sure he wants any. So, as Miss Freed explained, the two had some big decisions to make. The girls went out to play, leaving Miss Freed deep in thought.

Circle.

Marriage is not something you should . . .

    do.   even think about.   rush into.   ever want.   consider lightly.

Check.

Miss Freed and Sam must discuss the following before setting a date:

- ☐ Hairy the cat
- ☐ Rover the dog
- ☐ where to live
- ☐ what to buy
- ☐ children
- ☐ a wedding dress

Underline.

Marriage is a big and important . . .

    step.   commitment.   commandment.   question.

Write.

List five things you should consider when you get married. _____

_____

_____

•SOMETHING EXTRA•

What do you want to do after you graduate from high school?

Who Will Win?

Mrs. Farrell is the principal of Dukwilma. She is a good principal and all of the students at Dukwilma love her. She's tough but fair.

Miss Freed's sixth graders nominated Mrs. Farrell as Principal of the Year in the country-wide contest sponsored by the White House. To do this, they had to write an essay. If Mrs. Farrell wins, she, Miss Freed, and the whole sixth-grade class will get to go to Washington, D.C. to see the White House and have dinner with the President. How exciting! Miss Freed's students feel sure she will win.

In the essay, the sixth graders told how fair Mrs. Farrell is to all students. They described how Mrs. Farrell always listens to both sides of an issue before making a decision. They also wrote that the students at Dukwilma like her because she relates well to them. The students told how she wore jeans to their pizza party and even knew the latest dance steps. They also mentioned how well-respected she is in the community. Mrs. Farrell involves the school with community businesses and organizations as much as possible by implementing programs such as recycling and neighborhood clean-ups. She also arranges class tours of city buildings and organizations. All in all, the sixth graders think Mrs. Farrell is the greatest principal around.

Check.

Mrs. Farrell should win the contest if they are looking for someone who is . . .

☐ just.   ☐ interactive.   ☐ involved.   ☐ aloof.   ☐ apathetic.

Underline.

The students and Mrs. Farrell seem to have _____ respect for one another.

mutual   unconscious   unfaltering   repetitive   numerous

Write.

What are some qualities Mrs. Farrell has that you think will help her win? Why? _____

_____

_____

List some qualities you think a principal should have to win this award. _____

_____

•SOMETHING EXTRA•

Would you nominate your principal for this award? Why, or why not?

Tornado Trauma

Donald's dad is an inspector for an insurance agency. Donald is going with his dad to inspect a home damaged during a tornado. Donald is excited. He has never been with his dad on a job like this.

As Donald and his dad approach the house, Donald can't believe what he sees. There are trees and trash everywhere. He almost trips over an open photo album as he gets out of the car. He wonders where the smiling faces he sees in the photograph are now. The house Donald's dad is inspecting looks like all the others on the block. It has no roof, the windows are broken, and the yard is cluttered with debris. Donald jumps when a man, a woman, and a little boy, none of them wearing shoes, come out of the house. They tell Donald's father they are living in the basement because they have nowhere else to go. Donald recognizes the little boy as one of the faces in the photograph.

Donald and his father go in the house to look around. The inside of the house is battered and there are rips in the sofa and chairs. The man says they have lost all of their clothes, shoes, and many other belongings. Most importantly, however, the man wants his roof fixed. The nights are beginning to get cooler and he wants the house to be warm for his son. Donald feels sorry for the family. He is so glad they have insurance. He knows his dad will help them out.

Check.

Donald probably felt _____ when he left the damaged house.

☐ thankful   ☐ lucky   ☐ depressed   ☐ sympathetic   ☐ evasive

Circle.

The following probably made Donald feel sad:

his dad   a photo album   the roofless home   a little boy   a car   the battered house

Write.

What do you think the insurance company should pay for? Be specific. _____

_____

_____

Why is it good to have insurance? _____

_____

•SOMETHING EXTRA•

How many different kinds of insurance should you have? Why?

Answer Key

Reading for Understanding
Grade 6

Name ______________________ Skill: Predicting Outcomes

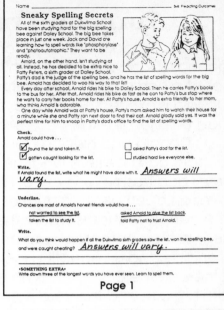

Sneaky Spelling Secrets

All of the sixth graders at Dukwilma School have been studying hard for the big spelling bee against Dailey School. The big bee takes place in just one week. Jack and David are learning how to spell words like "phosphorylase" and "photoautotrophic." They want to be ready.

Arnold, on the other hand, isn't studying at all. Instead, he has decided to be extra nice to Patty Peters, a sixth grader at Dailey School. Patty's dad is the judge of the spelling bee, and he has the list of spelling words for the big bee. Arnold has decided to woo his way to that list!

Every day after school, Arnold rides his bike to Dailey School. Then he carries Patty's books to the bus for her. After that, Arnold rides his bike as fast as he can to Patty's bus stop where he waits to carry her books home for her. At Patty's house, Arnold is extra friendly to her mom, who thinks Arnold is adorable.

One day while Arnold was at Patty's house, Patty's mom asked him to watch their house for a minute while she and Patty ran next door to find their cat. Arnold gladly said yes. It was the perfect time for him to snoop in Patty's dad's office to find the list of spelling words.

Check.
Arnold could have . . .

- [x] found the list and taken it.
- [x] gotten caught looking for the list.
- [ ] asked Patty's dad for the list.
- [ ] studied hard like everyone else.

Write.
If Arnold found the list, write what he might have done with it. *Answers will vary.*

Underline.
Chances are most of Arnold's honest friends would have . . .

<u>not wanted to see the list.</u> — taken the list to study it. — <u>asked Arnold to give the list back.</u> — told Patty not to trust Arnold.

Write.
What do you think would happen if all the Dukwilma sixth graders saw the list, won the spelling bee, and were caught cheating? *Answers will vary.*

•SOMETHING EXTRA•
Write down three of the longest words you have ever seen. Learn to spell them.

Page 1

Name ______________________ Skill: Predicting Outcomes

Dancing Dilemma

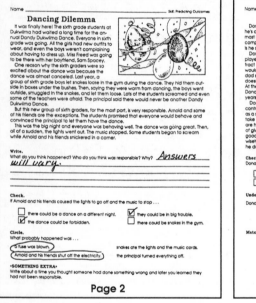

It was finally here! The sixth grade students at Dukwilma had waited a long time for the annual Dandy Dukwilma Dance. Everyone in sixth grade was going. All the girls had new outfits to wear, and even the boys weren't complaining about having to dress up. Miss Freed was going to be there with her boyfriend, Sam Spacey.

One reason why the sixth graders were so excited about the dance was because the dance was almost canceled. Last year, a group of sixth grade boys let snakes loose in the gym during the dance. They hid them outside in boxes under the bushes. Then, saying they were warm from dancing, the boys went outside, smuggled in the snakes, and let them loose. Lots of the students screamed and even some of the teachers were afraid. The principal said there would never be another Dandy Dukwilma Dance.

But this new group of sixth graders, for the most part, is very responsible. Arnold and some of his friends are the exceptions. The students promised that everyone would behave and convinced the principal to let them have the dance.

This was the big night and everyone was behaving well. The dance was going great. Then, all of a sudden, the lights went out. The music stopped. Some students began to scream while Arnold and his friends snickered in a corner.

Write.
What do you think happened? Who do you think was responsible? Why? *Answers will vary.*

Check.
If Arnold and his friends caused the lights to go off and the music to stop . . .

- [ ] there could be a dance on a different night.
- [x] the dance could be forbidden.
- [x] they could be in big trouble.
- [ ] there could be snakes in the gym.

Circle.
What probably happened was . . .

(a fuse was blown.) — (Arnold and his friends shut off the electricity.) — snakes ate the lights and the music cords. — the principal turned everything off.

•SOMETHING EXTRA•
Write about a time you thought someone had done something wrong and later you learned they had not been responsible.

Page 2

Name ______________________ Skill: Predicting Outcomes

Must We Move?

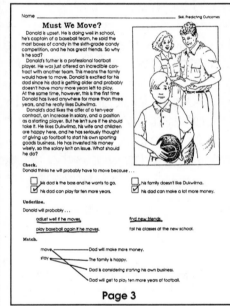

Donald is upset. He is doing well in school, he's captain of a baseball team, he sold the most boxes of candy in the sixth-grade candy competition, and he has great friends. So why is he sad?

Donald's father is a professional football player. He was just offered an incredible contract with another team. This means the family would have to move. Donald is excited for his dad since his dad is getting older and probably doesn't have many more years left to play. At the same time, however, this is the first time Donald has lived anywhere for more than three years, and he really likes Dukwilma.

Donald's dad likes the offer of a ten-year contract, an increase in salary, and a position as a starting player. But he isn't sure if he should take it. He likes Dukwilma, his wife and children are happy here, and he has seriously thought of giving up football to start his own sporting goods business. He has invested his money wisely, so the salary isn't an issue. What should he do?

Check.
Donald thinks he will probably have to move because . . .

- [ ] his dad is the boss and he wants to go.
- [x] his dad can play for ten more years.
- [ ] his family doesn't like Dukwilma.
- [x] his dad can make a lot more money.

Underline.
Donald will probably . . .

<u>adjust well if he moves.</u> — <u>play baseball again if he moves.</u> — <u>find new friends.</u> — fail his classes at the new school.

Match.

- move — Dad will make more money.
- stay — The family is happy.
- stay — Dad is considering starting his own business.
- move — Dad will get to play ten more years of football.

Page 3

Name ______________________ Skill: Character Analysis

Foreign Friends

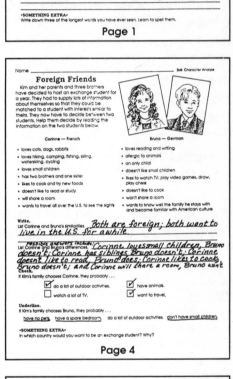

Kim and her parents and three brothers have decided to host an exchange student for a year. They had to supply lots of information about themselves so that they could be matched to a student with interests similar to theirs. They now have to decide between two students. Help them decide by reading the information on the two students below.

Corinne — French	Bruno — German
• loves cats, dogs, rabbits	• loves reading and writing
• loves hiking, camping, fishing, skiing, waterskiing, cycling	• allergic to animals
• loves small children	• an only child
• has two brothers and one sister	• doesn't like small children
• likes to cook and try new foods	• likes to watch TV, play video games, draw, play chess
• doesn't like to read or study	• doesn't like to cook
• will share a room	• won't share a room
• wants to travel all over the U.S. to see the sights	• wants to know well the family he stays with and become familiar with American culture

Write.
List Corinne and Bruno's similarities. *Both are foreign; both want to live in the U.S. for awhile.*

List Corinne and Bruno's differences. *Possible answers include: Corinne loves small children, Bruno doesn't; Corinne has siblings, Bruno doesn't; Corinne doesn't like to read, Bruno does; Corinne likes to cook, Bruno doesn't; and Corinne will share a room, Bruno won't*

Check.
If Kim's family chooses Corinne, they probably . . .

- [x] do a lot of outdoor activities.
- [ ] watch a lot of TV.
- [x] have animals.
- [x] want to travel.

Underline.
If Kim's family chooses Bruno, they probably . . .

<u>have no pets.</u> — <u>have a spare bedroom.</u> — do a lot of outdoor activities. — <u>don't have small children.</u>

•SOMETHING EXTRA•
In which country would you want to be an exchange student? Why?

Page 4

Name ______________________ Skill: Character Analysis

Morning Blues

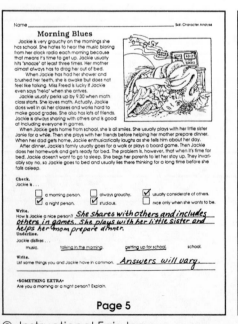

Jackie is very grouchy on the mornings she has school. She hates to hear the music blaring from her clock radio each morning because that means it's time to get up. Jackie usually hits "snooze" at least three times. Her mother almost always has to drag her out of bed.

When Jackie has had her shower and brushed her teeth, she is awake but does not feel like talking. Miss Freed is lucky if Jackie even says "hello" when she arrives.

Jackie usually perks up by 9:30 when math class starts. She loves math. Actually, Jackie does well in all her classes and works hard to make good grades. She also has lots of friends. Jackie is always sharing with others and is good at including everyone in games.

When Jackie gets home from school, she is all smiles. She usually plays with her little sister Janie for a while. Then she plays with her friends before helping her mother prepare dinner. When her dad gets home, Jackie enthusiastically laughs as she tells him about her day.

After dinner, Jackie's family usually goes for a walk or plays a board game. Then Jackie does her homework and gets ready for bed. The problem is, however, that when it's time for bed, Jackie doesn't want to go to sleep. She begs her parents to let her stay up. They invariably say no, so Jackie goes to bed and usually lies there thinking for a long time before she falls asleep.

Check.
Jackie is . . .

- [ ] a morning person.
- [x] a night person.
- [ ] always grouchy.
- [x] studious.
- [x] usually considerate of others.
- [ ] nice only when she wants to be.

Write.
How is Jackie a nice person? *She shares with others and includes others in games. She plays with her little sister and helps her mom prepare dinner.*

Underline.
Jackie dislikes . . .

music. — <u>talking in the morning.</u> — <u>getting up for school.</u> — school.

Write.
List some things you and Jackie have in common. *Answers will vary.*

•SOMETHING EXTRA•
Are you a morning or a night person? Explain.

Page 5

Name ______________________ Skill: Character Analysis

This Is Love!

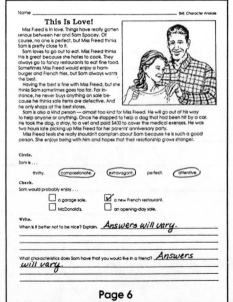

Miss Freed is in love. Things have really gotten serious between her and Sam Spacey. Of course, no one is perfect, but Miss Freed thinks Sam is pretty close to it.

Sam loves to go out to eat. Miss Freed thinks this is great because she hates to cook. They always go to fancy restaurants to eat fine food. Sometimes Miss Freed would enjoy a hamburger and French fries, but Sam always wants the best.

Having the best is fine with Miss Freed, but she thinks Sam sometimes goes too far. For instance, he never buys anything on sale because he thinks sale items are defective. And he only shops at the best stores.

Sam is also a kind person — almost too kind for Miss Freed. He will go out of his way to help anyone or anything. Once he stopped to help a dog that had been hit by a car. He took the dog, a stray, to a vet and paid $400 to cover the medical exenses. He was two hours late picking up Miss Freed for her parents' anniversary party.

Miss Freed feels she really shouldn't complain about Sam because he is such a good person. She enjoys being with him and hopes that their relationship grows stronger.

Circle.
Sam is . . .

thrifty. — (compassionate.) — (extravagant.) — perfect. — (attentive.)

Check.
Sam would probably enjoy . . .

- [ ] a garage sale.
- [ ] McDonald's.
- [x] a new French restaurant.
- [ ] an opening-day sale.

Write.
When is it better not to be nice? Explain. *Answers will vary.*

What characteristics does Sam have that you would like in a friend? *Answers will vary.*

Page 6

Name ______________________ Skill: Character Analysis

Being New Is No Fun

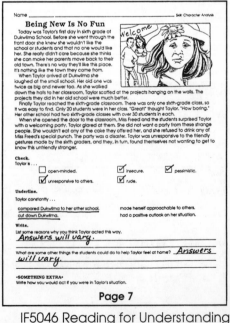

Today was Taylor's first day in sixth grade at Dukwilma School. Before she went through the front door she knew she wouldn't like the school or students and that no one would like her. She really didn't care because she thinks she can make her parents move back to their old town. There's no way they'll like this place. It's nothing like the town they came from.

When Taylor arrived at Dukwilma she laughed at the small school. Her old one was twice as big and newer too. As she walked down the halls to her classroom, Taylor scoffed at the projects hanging on the walls. The projects they did in her old school were much better.

Finally Taylor reached the sixth-grade classroom. There was only one sixth-grade class, so it was easy to find. Only 20 students were in her class. "Great!" thought Taylor. "How boring." Her other school had two sixth-grade classes with over 30 students in each.

When she opened the door to the classroom, Miss Freed and the students surprised Taylor with a welcoming party. Taylor glared at them. She did not want a party from these strange people. She wouldn't eat any of the cake they offered her, and she refused to drink any of Miss Freed's special punch. The party was a disaster. Taylor was unresponsive to the friendly gestures made by the sixth graders, and they, in turn, found themselves not wanting to get to know this unfriendly stranger.

Check.
Taylor is . . .

- [ ] open-minded.
- [x] unresponsive to others.
- [x] insecure.
- [x] rude.
- [x] pessimistic.

Underline.
Taylor constantly . . .

<u>compared Dukwilma to her other school.</u> — <u>cut down Dukwilma.</u> — made herself approachable to others. — had a positive outlook on her situation.

Write.
List some reasons why you think Taylor acted this way. *Answers will vary.*

What are some other things the students could do to help Taylor feel at home? *Answers will vary.*

•SOMETHING EXTRA•
Write how you would act if you were in Taylor's situation.

Page 7

Name ______________________ Skill: Cause and Effect

Look Out, It's Gonna Blow!

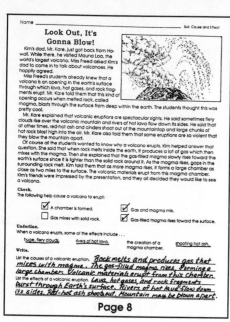

Kim's dad, Mr. Kare, just got back from Hawaii. While there, he visited Mauna Loa, the world's largest volcano. Miss Freed asked Kim's dad to come in to talk about volcanoes. He happily agreed.

Miss Freed's students already knew that a volcano is an opening in the earth's surface through which lava, hot gases, and rock fragments erupt. Mr. Kare told them that this kind of opening occurs when melted rock, called magma, blasts through the surface from deep within the earth. The students thought this was pretty cool.

Mr. Kare explained that volcanic eruptions are spectacular sights. He said sometimes fiery clouds rise over the volcanic mountain and rivers of hot lava flow down its sides. He said that at other times, red-hot ash and cinders shoot out of the mountaintop and large chunks of hot rock blast high into the air. Mr. Kare also told them that some eruptions are so violent that they blow the mountain apart.

Of course all the students wanted to know why a volcano erupts. Kim helped answer that question. She said that when rock melts inside the earth, it produces a lot of gas which then mixes with the magma. Then she explained that the gas-filled magma slowly rises toward the earth's surface since it is lighter than the solid rock around it. As the magma rises, gaps in the surrounding rock melt. Kim told them that as more magma rises, it forms a large chamber as close as two miles to the surface. The volcanic materials erupt from this magma chamber. Kim's friends were impressed by the presentation, and they all decided they would like to see a volcano.

Check.
The following help cause a volcano to erupt:

- [x] A chamber is formed.
- [ ] Gas mixes with solid rock.
- [x] Gas and magma mix.
- [x] Gas-filled magma rises toward the surface.

Underline.
When a volcano erupts, some of the effects include . . .
huge, fiery clouds. (underlined) rivers of hot lava. (underlined) the creation of a magma chamber. shooting hot ash. (underlined)

Write.
List the causes of a volcanic eruption. *Rock melts and produces gas that mixes with magma. The gas-filled magma rises, forming a large chamber. Volcanic materials erupt from this chamber.*
List the effects of a volcanic eruption. *Lava, hot gases, and rock fragments burst through Earth's surface. Rivers of hot lava flow down its sides. Red-hot ash shoots out. Mountain may be blown apart.*

Page 8

Name ______________________ Skill: Cause and Effect

Earthquakes

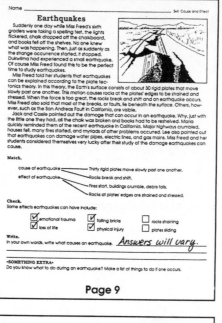

Suddenly one day while Miss Freed's sixth graders were taking a spelling test, the lights flickered, chalk dropped off the chalkboard, and books fell off the shelves. No one knew what was happening. Then, just as suddenly as the strange occurrence started, it stopped. Dukwilma had experienced a small earthquake. Of course Miss Freed found this to be the perfect time to study earthquakes.

Miss Freed told her students that earthquakes can be explained according to the plate tectonics theory. In this theory, the Earth's surface consists of about 30 rigid plates that move slowly past one another. This motion causes rocks at the plates' edges to be strained and stressed. When the force is too great, the rocks break and shift and an earthquake occurs. Miss Freed also said that most of the breaks, or faults, lie beneath the surface. Others, however, such as the San Andreas Fault in California, are visible.

Jack and Cassie pointed out the damage that can occur in an earthquake. Why, just with the little one they had, all the chalk was broken and books had to be reshelved. Maria quickly reminded them of the recent earthquake in California. Major highways crumbled, houses fell, many fires started, and myriads of other problems occurred. Lee also pointed out that earthquakes can damage water pipes, electric lines, and gas mains. Miss Freed and her students considered themselves very lucky after their study of the damage earthquakes can cause.

Match.
cause of earthquake — Thirty rigid plates move slowly past one another.
effect of earthquake — Rocks break and shift.
Fires start, buildings crumble, debris falls.
Rocks at plates' edges are strained and stressed.

Check.
Some effects earthquakes can have include:

- [x] emotional trauma
- [x] loss of life
- [x] falling bricks
- [x] physical injury
- [ ] rocks straining
- [ ] plates sliding

Write.
In your own words, write what causes an earthquake. *Answers will vary.*

•SOMETHING EXTRA•
Do you know what to do during an earthquake? Make a list of things to do if one occurs.

Page 9

Name ______________________ Skill: Cause and Effect

Celebrate 6th Graders

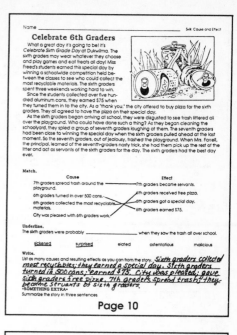

What a great day it's going to be! It's *Celebrate Sixth Grade Day* at Dukwilma. The sixth graders may wear whatever they choose and play games and eat treats all day! Miss Freed's students earned this special day by winning a schoolwide competition held between the classes to see who could collect the most recyclable materials. The sixth graders spent three weekends working hard to win.

Since the students collected over five hundred aluminum cans, they earned $75 when they turned them in to the city. As a "thank you," the city offered to buy pizza for the sixth graders. They all agreed to have the pizza on their special day.

As the sixth graders began arriving at school, they were disgusted to see trash littered all over the playground. Who could have done such a thing? As they began cleaning the schoolyard, they spied a group of seventh graders laughing at them. The seventh graders had been close to winning the special day when the sixth graders pulled ahead at the last moment. So the seventh graders, out of jealousy, trashed the playground. When Mrs. Farrell, the principal, learned of the seventh-graders nasty trick, she had them pick up the rest of the litter and act as servants of the sixth graders for the day. The sixth graders had the best day ever.

Match.

Cause	Effect
7th graders spread trash around the playground.	7th graders became servants.
6th graders turned in over 500 cans.	6th graders received free pizza.
6th graders collected the most recyclable materials.	6th graders got a special day.
City was pleased with 6th graders work.	6th graders earned $75.

Underline.
The sixth graders were probably ______________ when they saw the trash all over school.
sickened (underlined) surprised (underlined) elated ostentatious malicious

Write.
List as many causes and resulting effects as you can from the story. *Sixth graders collected most recyclables; they earned a special day. Sixth graders turned in 500 cans; earned $75. City was pleased; gave sixth graders free pizza. 7th graders spread trash; they became servants of sixth graders.*

•SOMETHING EXTRA•
Summarize the story in three sentences

Page 10

Name ______________________ Skill: Similarities and Differences

What's the Difference?

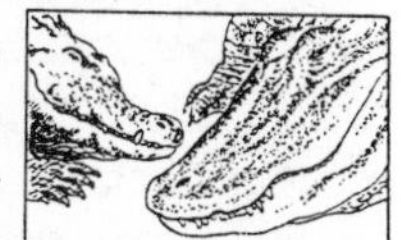

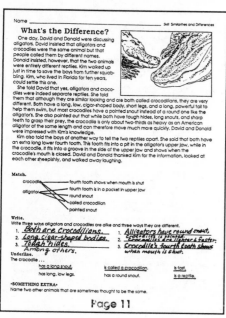

One day, David and Donald were discussing alligators. David insisted that alligators and crocodiles were the same animal but that people called them by different names. Donald insisted, however, that the two animals were entirely different reptiles. Kim walked up just in time to save the boys from further squabbling. Kim, who lived in Florida for ten years, could settle this one.

She told David that yes, alligators and crocodiles were indeed separate reptiles. She told them that although they are similar looking and are both called crocodilians, they are very different. Both have a long, low, cigar-shaped body, short legs, and a long, powerful tail to help them swim, but most crocodiles have a pointed snout instead of a round one like the alligator's. She also pointed out that while both have tough hides, long snouts, and sharp teeth to grasp their prey, the crocodile is only about two-thirds as heavy as an American alligator of the same length and can therefore move much more quickly. David and Donald were impressed with Kim's knowledge.

Kim also told the boys of another way to tell the two reptiles apart. She said that both have an extra long lower fourth tooth. This tooth fits into a pit in the alligator's upper jaw, while in the crocodile, it fits into a groove in the side of the upper jaw and shows when the crocodile's mouth is closed. David and Donald thanked Kim for the information, looked at each other sheepishly, and walked away laughing.

Match.
crocodile — fourth tooth shows when mouth is shut
alligator — fourth tooth is in a pocket in upper jaw
round snout
called crocodilian
pointed snout

Write.
Write three ways alligators and crocodiles are alike and three ways they are different.

1. *Both are crocodilians.*
2. *Long, cigar-shaped bodies.*
3. *Tough hides.* *Among others.*

1. *Alligators have round snout, crocodiles pointed.*
2. *Crocodiles are lighter & faster.*
3. *Crocodile's fourth tooth shows when mouth is shut.*

Underline.
The crocodile . . .
has a long snout. (underlined) is called a crocodilian. (underlined) is fast. (underlined)
has long, low legs. has a round snout. is a reptile. (underlined)

•SOMETHING EXTRA•
Name two other animals that are sometimes thought to be the same.

Page 11

Name ______________________ Skill: Similarities and Differences

An Exciting Exchange

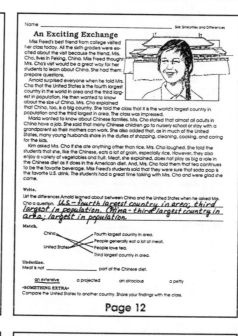

Miss Freed's best friend from college visited her class today. All the sixth graders were excited about the visit because the friend, Mrs. Cho, lives in Peking, China. Miss Freed thought Mrs. Cho's visit would be a great way for her students to learn about China. She had them prepare questions.

Arnold surprised everyone when he told Mrs. Cho that the United States is the fourth largest country in the world in area and the third largest in population. He then wanted to know about the size of China. Mrs. Cho explained that China, too, is a big country. She told the class that it is the world's largest country in population and the third largest in area. The class was impressed.

Maria wanted to know about Chinese families. Mrs. Cho stated that almost all adults in China have a job. She said that many Chinese children go to nursery school or stay with a grandparent so their mothers can work. She also added that, as in much of the United States, many young husbands share in the duties of shopping, cleaning, cooking, and caring for the kids.

Kim asked Mrs. Cho if she ate anything other than rice. Mrs. Cho laughed. She told the students that she, like the Chinese, eats a lot of grain, especially rice. However, they also enjoy a variety of vegetables and fruit. Meat, she explained, does not play as big a role in the Chinese diet as it does in the American diet. And, Mrs. Cho told them that tea continues to be the favorite beverage. Miss Freed's students said that they were sure that soda pop is the favorite U.S. drink. The students had a great time talking with Mrs. Cho and were glad she came.

Write.
List the differences Arnold learned about between China and the United States when he asked Mrs. Cho a question. *U.S.–fourth largest country in area; third largest in population. China–third largest country in area; largest in population.*

Match.
China — Fourth largest country in area.
United States — People generally eat a lot of meat.
People love tea.
Third largest country in area.

Underline.
Meat is not ______________ part of the Chinese diet.
an extensive (underlined) a projected an atrocious a petty

•SOMETHING EXTRA•
Compare the United States to another country. Share your findings with the class.

Page 12

Name ______________________ Skill: Similarities and Differences

Civilization Similarities

For the past month, the sixth graders at Dukwilma have been studying ancient civilizations. So far, they have learned about the ancient Greeks and Romans. The students were surprised at how interesting both civilizations were. They decided to teach the fifth graders about the ancient civilizations. Below are some of the things they told them.

Although both civilizations began over two thousand years ago, Greek civilization is older. It began around 2000 B.C. Legend says Roman civilization began in 753 B.C. Ancient Greece is known as the birthplace of Western civilization. The early Greeks made many advancements in government, science, philosophy, and the arts that influence our lives today.

Ancient Romans also had an enormous impact on the development of Western civilization. It was the Roman principles of justice and the Roman political system which shaped the formation of governments in the United States. Their roads, bridges, and aqueducts have also had an impact on the way many of these things are built in our country today.

In ancient Greece, civilization developed chiefly in small city-states. These consisted of a city or town and the surrounding villages and farmland. Ancient Rome, however, imposed central authority on big areas while still keeping local government. Roman rule gradually spread over all the lands bordering the Mediterranean Sea.

The fifth graders wanted the sixth graders to tell them more about the ancient civilizations of Greece and Rome. But the sixth graders stopped and told them they would have to wait to find out more on their own.

Write.
List the similarities and differences between ancient Greece and Rome.

Similarities
1. *Both began in B.C. years.*
2. *Both influenced our society.*
3. *"still influence us today."*

Differences *Include:*
1. *Rome began in 753; Greece around 2000.*
2. *Greece developed in city-states.*
3. *Greece known as birthplace of Western civilization.*

Match.
Ancient Greece — applied central authority on large areas.
Ancient Rome — built impressive aqueducts and bridges.
developed in city-states.
had an impact on the U.S.

Circle.
Ancient Rome and Greece were ______________ in helping make the U.S. what it is today.
preemptive possessive influential (circled) irrevocable

•SOMETHING EXTRA•
What is the oldest civilization? Where did it begin?

Page 13

Name ______________________ Skill: Similarities and Differences

People as Presidents

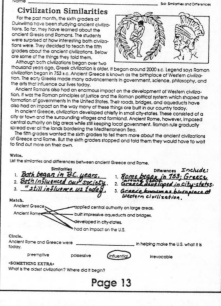

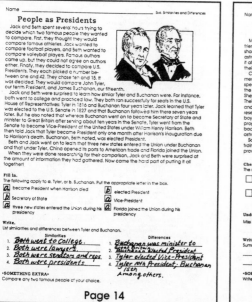

Jack and Beth spent several hours trying to decide which two famous people they wanted to compare. First, they thought they would compare famous athletes. Jack wanted to compare football players, and Beth wanted to compare volleyball players. Famous authors came up, but they could not agree on authors either. Finally, they decided to compare U.S. Presidents. They each picked a number between one and 42. They chose ten and 15. It was decided. They would compare John Tyler, our tenth President, and James Buchanan, our fifteenth.

Jack and Beth were surprised to learn how similar Tyler and Buchanan were. For instance, both went to college and practiced law. They both ran successfully for seats in the U.S. House of Representatives: Tyler in 1816 and Buchanan four years later. Jack learned that Tyler was elected to the U.S. Senate in 1827 and that Buchanan followed him there seven years later. But he also noted that whereas Buchanan went on to become Secretary of State and minister to Great Britain after serving about ten years in the Senate, Tyler went from the Senate to become Vice-President of the United States under William Henry Harrison. Beth then told Jack that Tyler became President only one month after Harrison's inauguration due to Harrison's death. Buchanan, Beth noted, was elected President.

Beth and Jack went on to learn that three new states entered the Union under Buchanan and that under Tyler, China opened its ports to American trade and Florida joined the Union.

When they were done researching for their comparison, Jack and Beth were surprised at the amount of information they had gathered. Now came the hard part of putting it all together!

Fill in.
The following apply to a. Tyler, or b. Buchanan. Put the appropriate letter in the box.

- *a* became President when Harrison died
- *b* Secretary of State
- *b* three new states entered the Union during his presidency
- *b* elected President
- *a* Vice-President
- *a* Florida joined the Union during his presidency

Write.
List similarities and differences between Tyler and Buchanan.

Similarities
1. *Both went to college.*
2. *Both were lawyers.*
3. *Both were senators and reps.*
4. *Both were presidents.*

Differences
1. *Buchanan was minister to Great Britain.*
2. *Buchanan elected President*
3. *Tyler elected Vice-President*
4. *Tyler 10th President; Buchanan 15th* *Among others.*

•SOMETHING EXTRA•
Compare any two famous people of your choice.

Page 14

Name ______________________ Skill: Main Idea

Miss Freed's Fascinating Friend

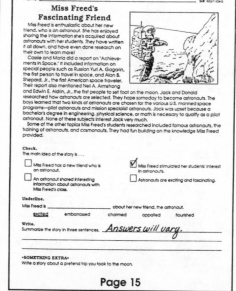

Miss Freed is enthusiastic about her new friend, who is an astronaut. She has enjoyed sharing the information she's acquired about astronauts with her students. They have written it all down, and have even done research on their own to learn more!

Cassie and Maria did a report on "Achievements in Space." It included information on special people such as Russian Yuri A. Gagarin, the first person to travel in space, and Alan B. Shepard, Jr., the first American space traveler. Their report also mentioned Neil A. Armstrong and Edwin E. Aldrin, Jr., the first people to set foot on the moon. Jack and Donald researched how astronauts are selected. They hope someday to become astronauts. The boys learned that two kinds of astronauts are chosen for the various U.S. manned space programs—pilot astronauts and mission specialist astronauts. Jack was upset because a bachelor's degree in engineering, physical science, or math is necessary to qualify as a pilot astronaut. None of these subjects interest Jack very much.

Some of the other topics Miss Freed's students researched included famous astronauts, the training of astronauts, and cosmonauts. They had fun building on the knowledge Miss Freed provided.

Check.
The main idea of the story is . . .

- [ ] Miss Freed has a new friend who is an astronaut.
- [ ] An astronaut shared interesting information about astronauts with Miss Freed's class.
- [x] Miss Freed stimulated her students' interest in astronauts.
- [ ] Astronauts are exciting and fascinating.

Underline.
Miss Freed is ______________ about her new friend, the astronaut.
excited (underlined) embarrassed charmed appalled flourished

Write.
Summarize the story in three sentences. *Answers will vary.*

•SOMETHING EXTRA•
Write a story about a pretend trip you took to the moon.

Page 15

Name ______________________ Skill: Main Idea

Family Tree Time

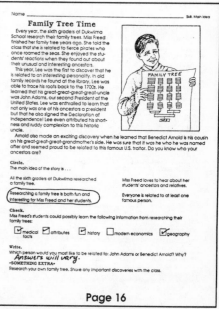

Every year, the sixth graders at Dukwilma School research their family trees. Miss Freed finished her family tree years ago. She told the class that she is related to fierce pirates who once roamed the seas. She enjoyed the students' reactions when they found out about their unusual and interesting ancestors.

This year, Lee was the first to discover that he is related to an interesting personality. In old family records he found at the library, Lee was able to trace his roots back to the 1700s. He learned that his great-great-great-great-uncle was John Adams, our second President of the United States. Lee was enthralled to learn that not only was one of his ancestors a president but that he also signed the Declaration of Independence! Lee even attributed his shortness and ruddy complexion to this historic uncle.

Arnold also made an exciting discovery when he learned that Benedict Arnold is his cousin on his great-great-great-grandmother's side. He was sure that it was he who he was named after and seemed proud to be related to this famous U.S. traitor. Do you know who your ancestors are?

Circle.
The main idea of the story is . . .
All the sixth graders at Dukwilma researched a family tree.
Miss Freed loves to hear about her students' ancestors and relatives.
Researching a family tree is both fun and interesting for Miss Freed and her students. (circled)
Everyone is related to at least one famous person.

Check.
Miss Freed's students could possibly learn the following information from researching their family trees:

- [x] medical facts
- [x] attributes
- [x] history
- [ ] modern economics
- [x] geography

Write.
Which person would you most like to be related to: John Adams or Benedict Arnold? Why?
Answers will vary.

•SOMETHING EXTRA•
Research your own family tree. Share any important discoveries with the class.

Page 16

Name ______________________ Skill: Main Idea

Brainy Information

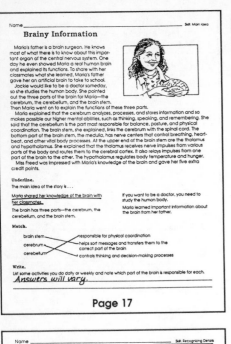

Maria's father is a brain surgeon. He knows most of what there is to know about this important organ of the central nervous system. One day he even showed Maria a real human brain and explained its functions. To share with her classmates what she learned, Maria's father gave her an artificial brain to take to school.

Jackie would like to be a doctor someday, so she studies the human body. She pointed out the three parts of the brain for Maria—the cerebrum, the cerebellum, and the brain stem. Then Maria went on to explain the functions of these three parts.

Maria explained that the cerebrum analyzes, processes, and stores information and so makes possible our higher mental abilities, such as thinking, speaking, and remembering. She said that the cerebellum is the part most responsible for balance, posture, and physical coordination. The brain stem, she explained, links the cerebrum with the spinal cord. The bottom part of the brain stem, the medulla, has nerve centers that control breathing, heartbeat, and other vital body processes. At the upper end of the brain stem are the thalamus and hypothalamus. She explained that the thalamus receives nerve impulses from various parts of the body and routes them to the cerebral cortex. It also relays impulses from one part of the brain to the other. The hypothalamus regulates body temperature and hunger.

Miss Freed was impressed with Maria's knowledge of the brain and gave her five extra credit points.

Underline.
The main idea of the story is . . .

- Maria shared her knowledge of the brain with her classmates. (underlined)
- The brain has three parts—the cerebrum, the cerebellum, and the brain stem.
- If you want to be a doctor, you need to study the human body.
- Maria learned important information about the brain from her father.

Match.

- brain stem — helps sort messages and transfers them to the correct part of the brain
- cerebrum — controls thinking and decision-making processes
- cerebellum — responsible for physical coordination

Write.
List some activities you do daily or weekly and note which part of the brain is responsible for each.
Answers will vary.

Page 17

Name ______________________ Skill: Main Idea

Nutty Nutrition

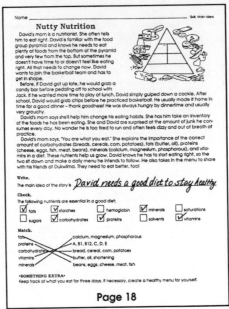

David's mom is a nutritionist. She often tells him to eat right. David is familiar with the food group pyramid and knows he needs to eat plenty of foods from the bottom of the pyramid and very few from the top. But sometimes he doesn't have time to or doesn't feel like eating right. All that needs to change now. David wants to join the basketball team and has to get in shape.

Before, if David got up late, he would grab a candy bar before pedaling off to school with Jack. If he wanted more time to play at lunch, David simply gulped down a cookie. After school, David would grab chips before he practiced basketball. He usually made it home in time for a good dinner – thank goodness! He was always hungry by dinnertime and usually very grouchy.

David's mom says she'll help him change his eating habits. She has him take an inventory of the foods he has been eating. She and David are surprised at the amount of junk he consumes every day. No wonder he is too tired to run and often feels dizzy and out of breath at practice.

David's mom says, "You are what you eat." She explains the importance of the correct amount of carbohydrates (breads, cereals, corn, potatoes), fats (butter, oil), proteins (cheese, eggs, fish, meat, beans), minerals (calcium, magnesium, phosphorous), and vitamins in a diet. These nutrients help us grow. David knows he has to start eating right, so the two sit down and make a daily menu he intends to follow. He also takes in the menu to share with his friends at Dukwilma. They need to eat better, too!

Write.
The main idea of the story is *David needs a good diet to stay healthy*

Check.
The following nutrients are essential in a good diet:

☑ fats ☑ starches ☐ hemoglobin ☑ minerals ☐ saturations
☐ sugars ☑ carbohydrates ☑ proteins ☐ solvents ☑ vitamins

Match.

- fats — butter, oil, shortening
- proteins — beans, eggs, cheese, meat, fish
- carbohydrates — bread, cereal, corn, potatoes
- vitamins — A, B1, B12, C, D, E
- minerals — calcium, magnesium, phosphorous

•**SOMETHING EXTRA**•
Keep track of what you eat for three days. If necessary, create a healthy menu for yourself.

Page 18

Name ______________________ Skill: Main Idea

Niagara Falls — Here We Come!

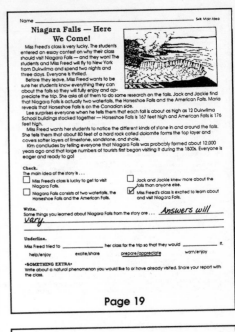

Miss Freed's class is very lucky. The students entered an essay contest on why their class should visit Niagara Falls — and they won! The students and Miss Freed will fly to New York from Dukwilma and spend two nights and three days. Everyone is thrilled.

Before they leave, Miss Freed wants to be sure her students know everything they can about the falls so they will fully enjoy and appreciate the trip. She asks all of them to do some research on the falls. Jack and Jackie find that Niagara Falls is actually two waterfalls, the Horseshoe Falls and the American Falls. Maria reveals that Horseshoe Falls is on the Canadian side.

Lee surprises everyone when he tells them that each fall is about as high as 12 Dukwilma School buildings stacked together — Horseshoe Falls is 167 feet high and American Falls is 176 feet high.

Miss Freed wants her students to notice the different kinds of stone in and around the falls. She tells them that about 80 feet of a hard rock called dolomite forms the top layer and covers softer layers of limestone, sandstone, and shale.

Kim concludes by telling everyone that Niagara Falls was probably formed about 12,000 years ago and that large numbers of tourists first began visiting it during the 1800s. Everyone is eager and ready to go!

Check.
The main idea of the story is . . .

☐ Miss Freed's class is lucky to get to visit Niagara Falls.
☐ Niagara Falls consists of two waterfalls, the Horseshoe Falls and the American Falls.
☐ Jack and Jackie knew more about the falls than anyone else.
☑ Miss Freed's class is excited to learn about and visit Niagara Falls.

Write.
Some things you learned about Niagara Falls from the story are . . . *Answers will vary.*

Underline.
Miss Freed tried to ____________ her class for the trip so that they would ____________ it.

help/enjoy excite/share prepare/appreciate (underlined) warn/enjoy

•**SOMETHING EXTRA**•
Write about a natural phenomenon you would like to or have already visited. Share your report with the class.

Page 19

Name ______________________ Skill: Recognizing Details

Flamingo Facts

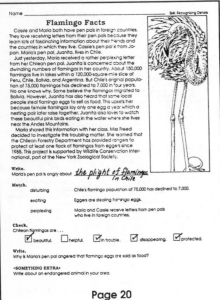

Cassie and Maria both have pen pals in foreign countries. They love receiving letters from their pen pals because they learn lots of fascinating information about their friends and the countries in which they live. Cassie's pen pal is from Japan. Maria's pen pal, Juanita, lives in Chile.

Just yesterday, Maria received a rather perplexing letter from her Chilean pen pal. Juanita is concerned about the dwindling numbers of flamingos in her country. About 150,000 flamingos live in lakes within a 120,000-square-mile slice of Peru, Chile, Bolivia, and Argentina. But Chile's original population of 75,000 flamingos has declined to 7,000 in four years. No one knows why. Some believe the flamingos migrated to Bolivia. However, Juanita has also heard that some local people steal flamingo eggs to sell as food. This upsets her because female flamingos lay only one egg a year which a nesting pair later raise together. Juanita also loves to watch these beautiful pink birds eating in the water where she lives near the Andes Mountains.

Maria shared this information with her class. Miss Freed decided to investigate this troubling matter. She learned that the Chilean Forestry Department has provided rangers to protect at least one flock of flamingos from eggers since 1985. This project is supported by Wildlife Conservation International, part of the New York Zoological Society.

Write.
Maria's pen pal is angry about *the plight of flamingos in Chile*

Match.

disturbing	Chile's flamingo population of 75,000 has declined to 7,000.
exciting	Eggers are stealing flamingo eggs.
perplexing	Maria and Cassie receive letters from pen pals who live in foreign countries.

Check.
Chilean flamingos are . . .

☑ beautiful. ☐ helpful. ☑ in trouble. ☑ disappearing. ☑ protected.

Write.
Why is Maria's pen pal angered that flamingo eggs are sold as food?

•**SOMETHING EXTRA**•
Write about an endangered animal in your area.

Page 20

Name ______________________ Skill: Recognizing Details

Lucky Lee

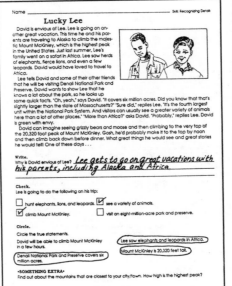

David is envious of Lee. Lee is going on another great vacation. This time he and his parents are traveling to Alaska to climb the majestic Mount McKinley, which is the highest peak in the United States. Just last summer, Lee's family went on a safari in Africa. Lee saw herds of elephants, fierce lions, and even a few leopards. David would have loved to travel to Africa.

Lee tells David and some of their other friends that he will be visiting Denali National Park and Preserve. David wants to show Lee that he knows a lot about the park, so he looks up some quick facts. "Oh, yeah," says David. "It covers six million acres. Did you know that that's slightly larger than the state of Massachusetts?" "Sure did," replies Lee. "It's the fourth largest unit within the National Park System. And visitors can usually see a greater variety of animals here than a lot of other places." "More than Africa?" asks David. "Probably," replies Lee. David is green with envy.

David can imagine seeing grizzly bears and moose and then climbing to the very top of the 20,320 foot peak of Mount McKinley. Gosh, he'd probably make it to the top by noon and then climb back down before dinner. What great things he would see and great stories he would tell! One of these days . . .

Write.
Why is David envious of Lee? *Lee gets to go on great vacations with his parents, including Alaska and Africa.*

Check.
Lee is going to do the following on his trip:

☐ hunt elephants, lions, and leopards. ☑ see a variety of animals.
☑ climb Mount McKinley. ☐ visit an eight-million-acre park and preserve.

Circle.
Circle the true statements.

- David will be able to climb Mount McKinley in a few hours.
- (circled) Lee saw elephants and leopards in Africa.
- (circled) Mount McKinley is 20,320 feet tall.
- (circled) Denali National Park and Preserve covers six million acres.

•**SOMETHING EXTRA**•
Find out about the mountains that are closest to your city/town. How high is the highest peak?

Page 21

Name ______________________ Skill: Recognizing Details

What a Whale Shark!

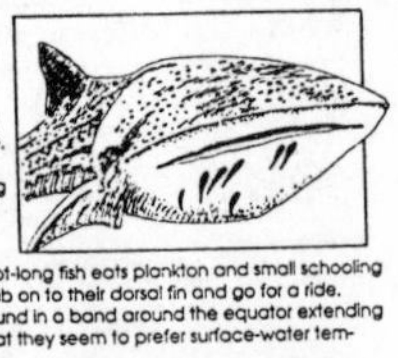

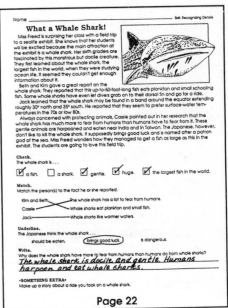

Miss Freed is surprising her class with a field trip to a sealife exhibit. She knows that her students will be excited because the main attraction at the exhibit is a whale shark. Her sixth graders are fascinated by this monstrous but docile creature. They first learned about the whale shark, the largest fish in the world, when they were studying ocean life. It seemed they couldn't get enough information about it.

Beth and Kim gave a great report on the whale shark. They reported that this up-to-50-foot-long fish eats plankton and small schooling fish. Some whale sharks have even let divers grab on to their dorsal fin and go for a ride.

Jack learned that the whale shark may be found in a band around the equator extending roughly 30° north and 35° south. He reported that they seem to prefer surface-water temperatures in the 70s or low 80s.

Always concerned with protecting animals, Cassie pointed out in her research that the whale shark has much more to fear from humans than humans have to fear from it. These gentle animals are harpooned and eaten near India and in Taiwan. The Japanese, however, don't like to kill the whale shark. It supposedly brings good luck and is named after a patron god of the sea. Miss Freed wonders how they managed to get a fish as large as this in the exhibit. The students are going to love this field trip.

Check.
The whale shark is . . .

☑ a fish. ☐ a shark. ☑ gentle. ☑ huge. ☑ the largest fish in the world.

Match.
Match the person(s) to the fact he or she reported.

- Kim and Beth — Whale sharks eat plankton and small fish.
- Cassie — The whale shark has a lot to fear from humans.
- Jack — Whale sharks like warmer waters.

Underline.
The Japanese think the whale shark . . .

should be eaten. (circled) brings good luck. is dangerous.

Write.
Why does the whale shark have more to fear from humans than humans do from whale sharks?
The whale shark is docile and gentle. Humans harpoon and eat whale sharks.

•**SOMETHING EXTRA**•
Make up a story about a ride you took on a whale shark.

Page 22

Name ______________________ Skill: Recognizing Details

Mrithi's Misfortune

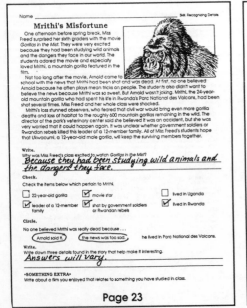

One afternoon before spring break, Miss Freed surprised her sixth graders with the movie *Gorillas in the Mist*. They were very excited because they had been studying wild animals and the dangers they face in our world. The students adored the movie and especially loved Mrithi, a mountain gorilla featured in the film.

Not too long after the movie, Arnold came to school with the news that Mrithi had been shot and was dead. At first, no one believed Arnold because he often plays mean tricks on people. The students also didn't want to believe the news because Mrithi was so sweet. But Arnold wasn't joking. Mrithi, the 24-year-old mountain gorilla who had spent his life in Rwanda's Parc National des Volcans, had been shot several times. Miss Freed and her whole class were shocked.

Mrithi's loss stunned observers, who feared that civil war would bring even more gorilla deaths and loss of habitat to the roughly 600 mountain gorillas remaining in the wild. The director of the park's veterinary center said she believed it was an accident, but she was very worried that it could happen again. It was unclear whether government soldiers or Rwandan rebels killed this leader of a 12-member family. All of Miss Freed's students hope that Ukwacumi, a 12-year-old male gorilla, will keep the surviving members together.

Write.
Why was Miss Freed's class excited to watch *Gorillas in the Mist*?
Because they had been studying wild animals and the dangers they face.

Check.
Check the items below which pertain to Mrithi.

☐ 22-year-old gorilla ☑ movie star ☐ lived in Uganda
☑ leader of a 12-member family ☑ shot by government soldiers or Rwandan rebels ☑ lived in Rwanda

Circle.
No one believed Mrithi was really dead because . . .

(circled) Arnold said it. (circled) the news was too sad. he lived in Parc National des Volcans.

Write.
Write down three details found in the story that help make it interesting.
Answers will vary.

•**SOMETHING EXTRA**•
Write about a film you enjoyed that relates to something you have studied in class.

Page 23

Name ______________________ Skill: Sequencing

Sorting Through a Horrible Mess

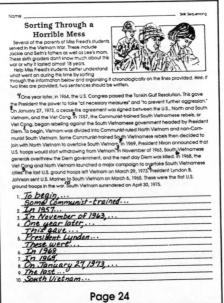

Several of the parents of Miss Freed's students served in the Vietnam War. These include Jackie and Beth's fathers as well as Lee's mom. These sixth graders don't know much about this war or why it lasted almost 18 years.

Help Miss Freed's students better understand what went on during this time by sorting through the information below and organizing it chronologically on the lines provided. **Hint:** If two lines are provided, two sentences should be written.

4 One year later, in 1964, the U.S. Congress passed the Tonkin Gulf Resolution. This gave the President the power to take "all necessary measures" and "to prevent further aggression." *8* On January 27, 1973, a cease-fire agreement was signed between the U.S., North and South Vietnam, and the Viet Cong. *2* In 1957, the Communist-trained South Vietnamese rebels, or Viet Cong, began rebelling against the South Vietnamese government headed by President Diem. *1* To begin, Vietnam was divided into Communist-ruled North Vietnam and non-Communist South Vietnam. Some Communist-trained South Vietnamese rebels then decided to join with North Vietnam to overtake South Vietnam. *7* In 1969, President Nixon announced that U.S. troops would start withdrawing from Vietnam. *3* In November of 1963, South Vietnamese generals overthrew the Diem government, and the next day Diem was killed. *6* In 1968, the Viet Cong and North Vietnam launched a major campaign to overtake South Vietnamese cities. *9* The last U.S. ground troops left Vietnam on March 29, 1973. *5* President Lyndon B. Johnson sent U.S. Marines to South Vietnam on March 6, 1965. These were the first U.S. ground troops in the war. *10* South Vietnam surrendered on April 30, 1975.

1. *To begin, . . .*
   Some Communist-trained . . .
2. *In 1957 . . .*
3. *In November of 1963, . . .*
4. *One year later, . . .*
   This gave . . .
5. *President Lyndon . . .*
   These were . . .
6. *In 1968,*
7. *In 1969,*
8. *On January 27, 1973, . . .*
9. *The last . . .*
10. *South Vietnam . . .*

Page 24

Name ______________________ Skill: Sequencing

Fantastic Philanthropist

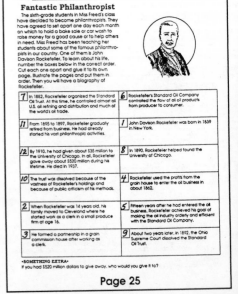

The sixth-grade students in Miss Freed's class have decided to become philanthropists. They have agreed to set apart one day each month on which to hold a bake sale or car wash to raise money for a good cause or to help others in need. Miss Freed has been teaching her students about some of the famous philanthropists in our country. One of them is John Davison Rockefeller. To learn about his life, number the boxes below in the correct order. Cut each one apart and glue it to its own page. Illustrate the pages and put them in order. Then you will have a biography of Rockefeller.

7 In 1882, Rockefeller organized the Standard Oil Trust. At this time, he controlled almost all U.S. oil refining and distribution and much of the world's oil trade.	*6* Rockefeller's Standard Oil Company controlled the flow of all oil products from producer to consumer.
11 From 1895 to 1897, Rockefeller gradually retired from business. He had already started his vast philanthropic activities.	*1* John Davison Rockefeller was born in 1839 in New York.
12 By 1910, he had given about $35 million to the University of Chicago. In all, Rockefeller gave away about $520 million during his lifetime. He died in 1937.	*8* In 1890, Rockefeller helped found the University of Chicago.
10 The trust was dissolved because of the vastness of Rockefeller's holdings and because of public criticism of his methods.	*4* Rockefeller used the profits from the grain house to enter the oil business in about 1862.
2 When Rockefeller was 14 years old, his family moved to Cleveland where he started work as a clerk in a small produce firm at age 16.	*5* Fifteen years after he had entered the oil business, Rockefeller achieved his goal of making the oil industry orderly and efficient with the Standard Oil Company.
3 He formed a partnership in a grain commission house after working as a clerk.	*9* About two years later, in 1892, the Ohio Supreme Court dissolved the Standard Oil Trust.

•**SOMETHING EXTRA**•
If you had $520 million dollars to give away, who would you give it to?

Page 25

Name ______________________ Skill: Sequencing

Miss Freed's Special Day

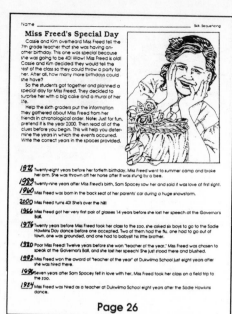

Cassie and Kim overheard Miss Freed tell the 7th grade teacher that she was having another birthday. This one was special because she was going to be 40! Wow! Miss Freed is old! Cassie and Kim decided they would tell the rest of the class so they could throw a party for her. After all, how many more birthdays could she have?

So the students got together and planned a special day for Miss Freed. They decided to surprise her with a big cake and a mural of her life.

Help the sixth graders put the information they gathered about Miss Freed from her friends in chronological order. **Note:** Just for fun, pretend it is the year 2000. Then read all of the clues before you begin. This will help you determine the years in which the events occurred. Write the correct years in the spaces provided.

1972 Twenty-eight years before her fortieth birthday, Miss Freed went to summer camp and broke her arm. She was thrown off her horse after it was stung by a bee.

1989 Twenty-nine years after Miss Freed's birth, Sam Spacey saw her and said it was love at first sight.

1960 Miss Freed was born in the back seat of her parents' car during a huge snowstorm.

2000 Miss Freed turns 40! She's over the hill!

1966 Miss Freed got her very first pair of glasses 14 years before she lost her speech at the Governor's Ball.

1976 Twenty years before Miss Freed took her class to the zoo, she asked six boys to go to the Sadie Hawkins Day dance before one accepted. Two of them had the flu, one had to go out of town, one was grounded, and one had to babysit his little brother.

1980 Poor Miss Freed! Twelve years before she won "teacher of the year," Miss Freed was chosen to speak at the Governor's Ball, and she lost her speech! She just stood there and blushed.

1992 Miss Freed won the award of "teacher of the year" at Dukwilma School just eight years after she was hired there.

1996 Seven years after Sam Spacey fell in love with her, Miss Freed took her class on a field trip to the zoo.

1984 Miss Freed was hired as a teacher at Dukwilma School eight years after the Sadie Hawkins dance.

Page 26

Name ______________________ Skill: Sequencing

Arnold's Awful Antics

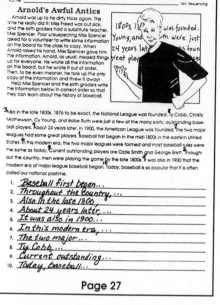

Arnold was up to his dirty tricks again. This time he really did it! Miss Freed was out sick, and the sixth graders had a substitute teacher, Miss Spencer. Poor unsuspecting Miss Spencer asked for a volunteer to write some information on the board for the class to copy. When Arnold raised his hand, Miss Spencer gave him the information. Arnold, as usual, messed things up for everyone. He wrote all the information on the board, but he wrote it out of order. Then, to be even meaner, he tore up the only copy of the information and threw it away!

Help Miss Spencer and the sixth graders write the information below in correct order so that they can learn about the history of baseball.

3 Also in the late 1800s, 1876 to be exact, the National League was founded. 8 Ty Cobb, Christy Mathewson, Cy Young, and Babe Ruth were just a few of the many early, outstanding baseball players. 4 About 24 years later, in 1900, the American League was founded. 7 The two major leagues had some great players. 1 Baseball first began in the mid-1800s in the eastern United States. 6 In this modern era, the two major leagues were formed and most baseball rules were the same as today. 9 Current outstanding players are Ozzie Smith and George Brett. 2 Throughout the country, men were playing the game by the late 1800s. 5 It was also in 1900 that the modern era of major league baseball began. 10 Today, baseball is so popular that it is often called our national pastime.

1. Baseball first began...
2. Throughout the country, ...
3. Also in the late 1800,
4. About 24 years later, ...
5. It was also in 1900...
6. In this modern era, ...
7. The two major...
8. Ty Cobb, ...
9. Current outstanding...
10. Today, baseball...

Page 27

Name ______________________ Skill: Classification

Very Interesting Vertebrates

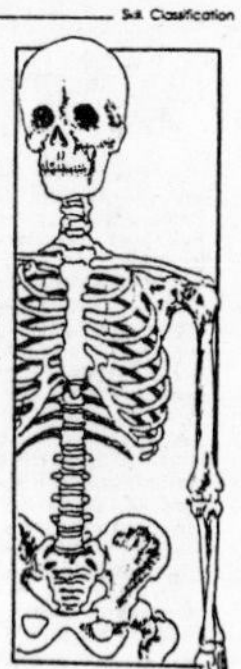

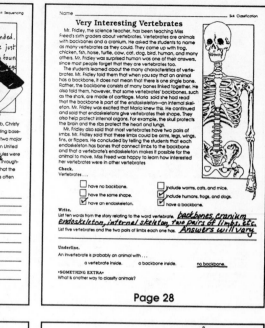

Mr. Fridley, the science teacher, has been teaching Miss Freed's sixth graders about vertebrates. Vertebrates are animals with backbones and a cranium. He asked the students to name as many vertebrates as they could. They came up with frog, chicken, fish, horse, turtle, cow, cat, dog, bird, human, and many others. Mr. Fridley was surprised human was one of their answers, since most people forget that they are vertebrates too.

The students learned about the many characteristics of vertebrates. Mr. Fridley told them that when you say that an animal has a backbone, it does not mean that there is one single bone. Rather, the backbone consists of many bones linked together. He also told them, however, that some vertebrates' backbones, such as the shark, are made of cartilage. Maria said she had read that the backbone is part of the *endoskeleton*—an internal skeleton. Mr. Fridley was excited that Maria knew this. He continued and said that endoskeletons give vertebrates their shape. They also help protect internal organs. For example, the skull protects the brain and the ribs protect the heart and lungs.

Mr. Fridley also said that most vertebrates have two pairs of limbs. Mr. Fridley said that these limbs could be arms, legs, wings, fins, or flippers. He concluded by telling the students that each endoskeleton has bones that connect limbs to the backbone and that a vertebrate's endoskeleton makes it possible for the animal to move. Miss Freed was happy to learn how interested her vertebrates were in other vertebrates

Check.

Vertebrates . . .

- [ ] have no backbone.
- [ ] have the same shape.
- [x] have an endoskeleton.
- [ ] include worms, cats, and mice.
- [x] include humans, frogs, and dogs.
- [x] have a backbone.

Write.

List ten words from the story relating to the word *vertebrate*. backbones, cranium endoskeleton, internal skeleton, two pairs of limbs, etc.

List five vertebrates and the two pairs of limbs each one has. Answers will vary.

Underline.

An invertebrate is probably an animal with . . .

a vertebrate inside.   a backbone inside.   <u>no backbone.</u>

•SOMETHING EXTRA•

What is another way to classify animals?

Page 28

Name ______________________ Skill: Classification

What's an Invertebrate?

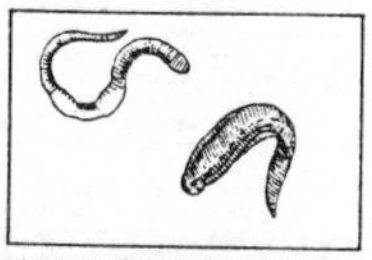

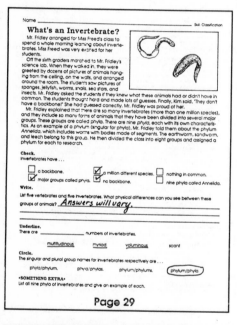

Mr. Fridley arranged for Miss Freed's class to spend a whole morning learning about invertebrates. Miss Freed was very excited for her students.

Off the sixth graders marched to Mr. Fridley's science lab. When they walked in, they were greeted by dozens of pictures of animals hanging from the ceiling, on the walls, and arranged around the room. The students saw pictures of sponges, jellyfish, worms, snails, sea stars, and insects. Mr. Fridley asked the students if they knew what these animals had or didn't have in common. The students thought hard and made lots of guesses. Finally, Kim said, "They don't have a backbone!" She had guessed correctly. Mr. Fridley was proud of her.

Mr. Fridley explained that there are so many invertebrates (more than one million species), and they include so many forms of animals that they have been divided into several major groups. These groups are called phyla. There are nine *phyla*, each with its own characteristics. As an example of a phylum (singular for phyla), Mr. Fridley told them about the phylum *Annelida*, which includes worms with bodies made of segments. The earthworm, sandworm, and leech belong to this group. He then divided the class into eight groups and assigned a phylum for each to research.

Check.

Invertebrates have . . .

- [ ] a backbone.
- [x] major groups called phyla.
- [x] a million different species.
- [x] no backbone.
- [ ] nothing in common.
- [ ] nine phyla called Annelida.

Write.

List five vertebrates and five invertebrates. What physical differences can you see between these groups of animals? Answers will vary.

Underline.

There are ______________ numbers of invertebrates.

<u>multitudinous</u>   <u>myriad</u>   <u>voluminous</u>   scant

Circle.

The singular and plural group names for invertebrates respectively are . . .

phyla/phylum.   phyla/phylas.   phylum/phylums.   (phylum/phyla.)

•SOMETHING EXTRA•

List all nine phyla of invertebrates and give an example of each.

Page 29

Name ______________________ Skill: Classification

You Snake!

Miss Freed's class has lately been having a great time in science class. Mr. Fridley makes science fun. Miss Freed easily guessed what her students studied today because of their jesting: "You snake!" "You low-lying lizard!" "See ya' later, alligator!" "After awhile, crocodile!" Miss Freed figured today was Reptile Day.

Miss Freed was right. Mr. Fridley told the students that reptiles are animals with dry, scaly skin that breathe by means of lungs. He then assigned each of the sixth graders one of the 6,000 or so kinds of reptiles and asked them to research ten facts about it. Then, each student had to pretend to be that reptile and call out clues about the animal. The students had fun guessing the correct reptiles.

When the game was over, Mr. Fridley asked the students which clues most of the reptiles had in common. The students thought about it and gradually came up with some answers. Donald remembered that they were cold-blooded — that is, their body temperature stays about the same as the temperature of their surroundings. Jack remembered that most reptiles that are active during the day have to keep moving from sunny to shady spots to avoid extremely high or low temperatures. Cassie and Lee both blurted out that reptiles in regions with harsh winters hibernate in the winter. Mr. Fridley was surprised at how much information the students had gathered.

Mr. Fridley then explained that there are four main groups of reptiles — lizards and snakes, turtles, crocodilians, and the tuatara — and that they live in various habitats on every continent except Antarctica. The sixth graders agreed that reptiles are pretty cool.

Match.

Reptiles — are cold-blooded.
Reptiles — avoid extremely high or low temperatures.

live on all continents.
hibernate in winter.

Write.

Explain what cold-blooded means and tell how it affects some reptile behavior. Cold-blooded means the body temperature stays about the same as the temperature of its surroundings. Some reptiles active during the day must move from sunny to shady spots to avoid extreme temperatures.

Circle.

Reptiles have many ______________ habitats.

similar   (variant)   parallel   distinguished

•SOMETHING EXTRA•

Write ten facts about a reptile of your choice.

Page 30

Name ______________________ Skill: Classification

Realistic or an Impression?

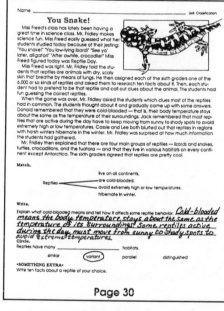

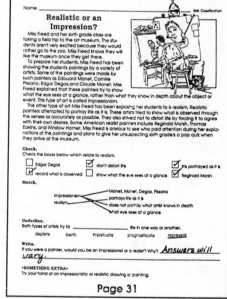

Miss Freed and her sixth grade class are taking a field trip to the art museum. The students aren't very excited because they would rather go to the zoo. Miss Freed knows they will like the museum once they get there.

To prepare her students, Miss Freed has been showing the students paintings by a variety of artists. Some of the paintings were made by such painters as Edouard Manet, Camille Pissarro, Edgar Degas, and Claude Monet. Miss Freed explained that these painters try to show what the eye sees at a glance, rather than what they know in depth about the object or event. This type of art is called *impressionism*.

The other type of art Miss Freed has been exposing her students to is *realism*. Realistic painters attempted to portray life as it is. These artists tried to show what is observed through the senses as accurately as possible. They also strived not to distort life by forcing it to agree with their own desires. Some American realist painters include Reginald Marsh, Thomas Eakins, and Winslow Homer. Miss Freed is anxious to see who paid attention during her explanations of the paintings and plans to give her unsuspecting sixth graders a pop quiz when they arrive at the museum.

Check.

Check the boxes below which relate to realism.

- [ ] Edgar Degas
- [x] record what is observed
- [x] don't distort life
- [ ] show what the eye sees at a glance
- [x] life portrayed as it is
- [x] Reginald Marsh

Match.

impressionism — Manet, Monet, Degas, Pissarro
impressionism — does not portray what artist knows in depth
impressionism — what eye sees at a glance
realism — portrays life as it is

Underline.

Both types of artists try to ______________ life in one way or another.

deplete   berth   impetuate   prognosticate   <u>represent</u>

Write.

If you were a painter, would you be an impressionist or a realist? Why? Answers will vary.

•SOMETHING EXTRA•

Try your hand at an impressionistic or realistic drawing or painting.

Page 31

Name ______________________ Skill: Following Directions

Listen! The Elephants Are Talking

Frequency - a count of the number of waves that pass a given point in a given period of time.

Miss Freed's class is <u>studying</u> <u>animals</u> that are in danger of <u>becoming</u> extinct. One day, Donald came to class with some <u>interesting</u> <u>information</u> on <u>elephants</u>. Donald read in a <u>magazine</u> that <u>elephants</u> do more than just roar, trumpet, or snort. Donald told his classmates that they also make sounds that human ears cannot hear.

Cassie wanted to know how humans would know about these sounds if they couldn't hear them. Donald told Cassie that a <u>biologist</u> named <u>Katherine</u> Payne found out about the sounds in 1984 while she was at a zoo. Donald said that Mrs. Payne felt the air around her throb as she observed the <u>elephants</u>. She thought that this could be low-<u>frequency</u> sounds made by the <u>elephants</u> that she could not hear. Donald pointed out that Mrs. Payne <u>hypothesized</u> that the newly <u>discovered</u> <u>elephant</u> sounds could travel over a much greater distance than an <u>elephant's</u> trumpet or roar.

Jack asked if Mrs. Payne's <u>hypothesis</u> was true. Donald told him that in 1986, Payne went to Africa to test her <u>hypothesis</u>. He said that she wondered if the <u>elephants</u> used the calls to locate each other in the vast <u>African</u> plains and forests. What Mrs. Payne learned was that <u>elephant's</u> foreheads flutter and their ears flap when they make low-<u>frequency</u> calls. These calls seemed to help the <u>elephants</u> find each other. Donald's friends and Miss Freed were impressed with his <u>information</u>.

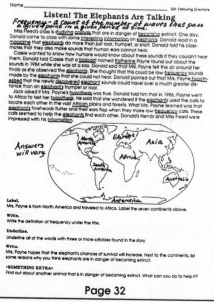

Answers will vary.

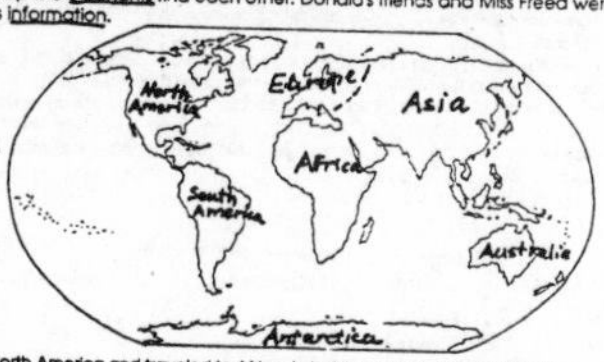

Label.

Mrs. Payne is from North America and traveled to Africa. Label the seven continents above.

Write.

Write the definition of frequency under the title.

Underline.

Underline all of the words with three or more syllables found in the story.

Write.

Mrs. Payne hopes that the elephant's chances of survival will increase. Next to the continents, list some reasons why you think elephants are in danger of becoming extinct.

•SOMETHING EXTRA•

Find out about another animal that is in danger of becoming extinct. What can you do to help it?

Page 32

Name ______________________ Skill: Following Directions

Mesopotamia

6,994 (depending on current year)

Miss <u>Freed's</u> <u>sixth</u> graders enjoyed learning about <u>ancient</u> Greece and Rome so much that she decided to teach them about Mesopotamia. She asked what they thought *Mesopotamia* was. Lee thought it sounded like a <u>fancy</u> soup. Jack thought it was a <u>deep</u>, <u>dark</u> hole out in space. Maria and Kim thought it was a <u>foreign</u> word. The rest of the students just wanted Miss Freed to hurry and tell them what it was.

Miss Freed explained that Mesopotamia was the region where the <u>world's</u> <u>first</u> civilization developed. She told them that the word means "between rivers." The heart of Mesopotamia was between the Tigris and Euphrates rivers. Today, parts of the countries of Syria, Turkey, and Iraq are located where Mesopotamia once thrived.

<u>Northern</u> Mesopotamia had a <u>mild</u> climate and received enough rain to enable crops to grow on parts of it. <u>Southern</u> Mesopotamia, often flooded by the Tigris and Euphrates rivers, provided <u>rich</u> farmland for its inhabitants. However, because of the <u>long</u>, <u>hot</u> summers, irrigation was necessary for agriculture.

In about 3500 B.C. <u>new</u> settlers arrived in a part of this region that became known as *Sumer*. The Sumerians, as they were called, built the <u>world's</u> <u>first</u> cities and developed the <u>first</u> civilization. They also invented the world's <u>first</u> system of writing called *cuneiform*.

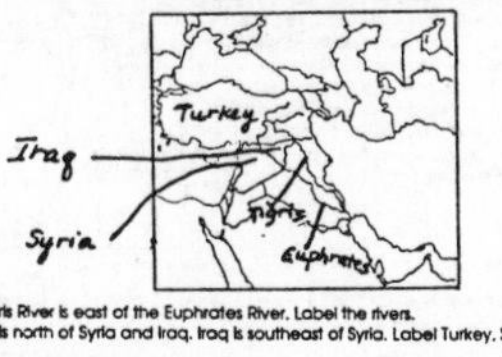

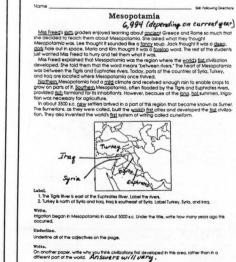

Label.

1. The Tigris River is east of the Euphrates River. Label the rivers.
2. Turkey is north of Syria and Iraq. Iraq is southeast of Syria. Label Turkey, Syria, and Iraq.

Write.

Irrigation began in Mesopotamia in about 5000 B.C. Under the title, write how many years ago this occurred.

Underline.

Underline all of the adjectives on the page.

Write.

On another paper, write why you think civilizations first developed in this area, rather than in a different part of the world. Answers will vary.

•SOMETHING EXTRA•

If you could take three things back in time to the first civilization, what you would take and why?

Page 33

Name ______________________ Skill: Following Directions

Plant Fun

Miss Freed's sixth graders are excited! They are the first class in Dukwilma to visit the new *Great Green Things Museum*. Lee's dad's company did some work on the museum. As a favor to him, his son's class is first to visit the museum.

The students think the museum is awesome. It's filled with some incredible plants, including some that eat insects! As they tour the museum, a guide explains photosynthesis. Most of the students have already studied photosynthesis, but it seems more real and understandable now that they are surrounded by exotic plants.

The guide explains that photosynthesis is the food-making process of green plants. This is the chief function of leaves. In this process, green plants use energy from light to combine carbon dioxide and water to make food. All our food comes from this important activity.

She further explains that plants perform another activity vital to our existence. They give off oxygen. We, in turn, "burn" the food by combining it with oxygen to release energy. Oxygen is used up and carbon dioxide is given off. This process of respiration is the reverse of photosynthesis. The cycle of photosynthesis and respiration maintains the Earth's natural balance of carbon dioxide and oxygen.

As the guide finishes her explanation, the students feel a renewed appreciation of plants. They tour the remainder of the museum, eager to tell their friends about what they saw and learned.

Write.

1. Write about the importance of oxygen to living things. Answers will vary. Include: Animals need oxygen to survive. Without oxygen, we would not be able to give off carbon dioxide, which plants need. Plants produce oxygen.
2. What do you think would happen if all the plants in the world began to die? Answers will vary. Include: we (all animals) would not have enough oxygen; natural balance of carbon dioxide and oxygen would be upset

Figure.

There are about 350,000 varieties of plants. About half of these are flowering. Using these figures, make up a math word problem and exchange it with a friend. Word problems will vary.

Draw.

Draw a picture depicting photosynthesis. Use an encyclopedia, if necessary.

•SOMETHING EXTRA•

What is your favorite plant. Why?

Page 34

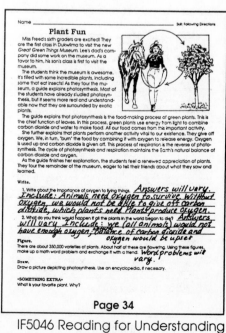

What a Slithering Mess!
Answers will vary.

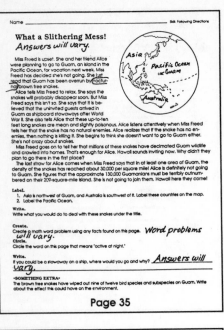

Miss Freed is upset. She and her friend Alice were planning to go to Guam, an island in the Pacific Ocean, for vacation next week. Miss Freed has decided she's not going. She just read that Guam has been overrun by nocturnal/brown tree snakes.

Alice tells Miss Freed to relax. She says the snakes will probably disappear soon. But Miss Freed says this isn't so. She says that it is believed that the uninvited guests arrived in Guam as shipboard stowaways after World War II. She also tells Alice that these up-to-ten feet long snakes are mean and slightly poisonous. Alice listens attentively when Miss Freed tells her that the snake has no natural enemies, then nothing is killing it. She begins to think she doesn't want to go to Guam either. She's not crazy about snakes.

Miss Freed goes on to relax. She says the snakes crawl into homes and crawled into homes. That's enough for Alice. Hawaii sounds inviting now. Why didn't they plan to go there in the first place?

The last straw for Alice comes when Miss Freed says that in at least one area of Guam, the density of the snakes has reached about 30,000 per square mile! Alice is definitely not going to Guam. She figures that the approximate 130,000 Guamanians must be terribly outnumbered on their 209-square-mile island. She is not going to join them. Hawaii here they come!

Label.
1. Asia is northwest of Guam, and Australia is southwest of it. Label these countries on the map.
2. Label the Pacific Ocean.

Write.
Write what you would do to deal with these snakes under the title.

Create.
Create a math word problem using any facts found on this page. *Word problems will vary.*

Circle.
Circle the word on this page that means "active at night."

Write.
If you could be a stowaway on a ship, where would you go and why? *Answers will vary.*

•SOMETHING EXTRA•
The brown tree snake has wiped out nine of twelve bird species and subspecies on Guam. Write about the effect this could have on the environment.

Page 35

Miss Freed's Trip on the Oregon Trail

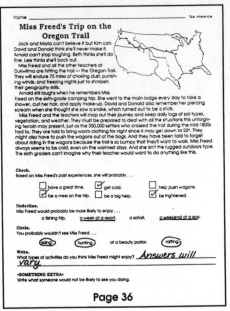

Jack and Maria can't believe it but Kim can. David and Donald think she'll never make it. Arnold can't stop laughing. Beth thinks she'll be fine. Lee thinks she'll back out.

Miss Freed and all the other teachers at Dukwilma are hitting the trail — the Oregon Trail. They will endure 75 miles of choking dust, punishing winds, and freezing nights just to sharpen their geography skills.

Arnold still laughs when he remembers Miss Freed on the sixth-grade camping trip. She went to the main lodge every day to take a shower, curl her hair, and apply make-up. David and Donald also remember her piercing scream when she thought she saw a snake, which turned out to be a stick.

Miss Freed and the teachers will map out their journey and keep daily logs of soil types, vegetation, and weather. They must be prepared to deal with all the situations this unforgiving terrain may present, just as the 350,000 settlers who crossed the trail during the mid-1800s had to. They are told to bring warm clothing for night since it may get down to 25°. They might also have to push the wagons out of the bogs. And they have been told to forget about riding in the wagons because the trail is so bumpy that they'll want to walk. Miss Freed always seems to be cold, even on the warmest days. And she isn't the rugged outdoors type. The sixth graders can't imagine why their teacher would want to do anything like this.

Check.
Based on Miss Freed's past experiences, she will probably . . .
- ☐ have a great time.
- ☑ get cold.
- ☐ help push wagons.
- ☐ be a mess on the trip.
- ☐ be a big help.
- ☑ be frightened.

Underline.
Miss Freed would probably be more likely to enjoy . . .
a fishing trip.   <u>a week at a resort.</u>   a safari.   <u>a weekend at a spa.</u>

Circle.
You probably wouldn't see Miss Freed . . .
(skiing)   (hunting)   at a beauty parlor.   (rafting)

Write.
What types of activities do you think Miss Freed might enjoy? *Answers will vary.*

•SOMETHING EXTRA•
Write what someone would not be likely to see you doing.

Page 36

The Duks vs. the Dodgers

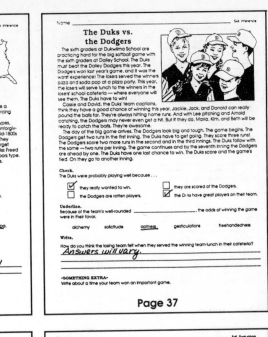

The sixth graders at Dukwilma School are practicing hard for the big softball game with the sixth graders at Dailey School. The Duks must beat the Dailey Dodgers this year. The Dodgers won last year's game, and it was the worst experience! The losers served the winners pizza and soda pop at a pizza party. This year, the losers will serve lunch to the winners in the losers' school cafeteria — where everyone will see them. The Duks have to win!

Cassie and David, the Duks' team captains, think they have a good chance of winning this year. Jackie, Jack, and Donald can really pound the balls this year. They're always hitting home runs. And with Lee pitching and Arnold catching, the Duks may never even get a hit. But if they do, Maria, Kim, and Beth will be ready to catch the balls. They're awesome.

The day of the big game arrives. The Dodgers look big and tough. The game begins. The Dodgers get two runs in the first inning. The Duks have to get going. They score three runs! The Dodgers score two more runs in the second and in the third innings. The Duks follow with the same — two runs per inning. The game continues and by the seventh inning the Dodgers are ahead by one. The Duks have one last chance to win. The Duks score and the game's tied. On they go to another inning.

Check.
The Duks were probably playing well because . . .
- ☑ they really wanted to win.
- ☐ they are scared of the Dodgers.
- ☐ the Dodgers are rotten players.
- ☑ the Duks have great players on their team.

Underline.
Because of the team's well-rounded _____ the odds of winning the game were in their favor.
alchemy   solicitude   <u>aptness</u>   gesticulations   freehandedness

Write.
How do you think the losing team felt when they served the winning team lunch in their cafeteria?
Answers will vary.

•SOMETHING EXTRA•
Write about a time your team won an important game.

Page 37

Fear of the Flood

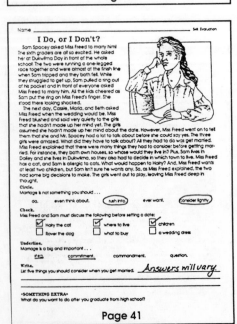

The whole town of Dukwilma is nervous. There has been so much rain lately that the people are afraid that their town will be flooded. Dukwilma hasn't flooded since 1972 when there was so much rain that Dukwilma Creek looked like a river and appeared to flow backwards! This was a sad time because many people's homes and businesses were destroyed by all the water. Those businesses that were spared were shut down for several weeks. While there's a chance that this might happen again.

Miss Freed's class decides to study floods to learn how damaging they could be to Dukwilma. Since Dukwilma is located on a river, the sixth graders are mainly concerned with river floods. They find that the common causes of river floods include too much rain and the sudden melting of snow or ice. Under these conditions, the sixth graders read, rivers may receive more than ten times as much water as their beds can hold. The students know that the river on which Dukwilma is situated is already approaching its capacity, and more rain is on its way. Thank goodness for the levee built after the 1972 flood. They hope it will hold the water back. Miss Freed's students are anxious to hear the weather forecast after lunch.

When the forecast does come on, it is as the students have feared. It is predicted that Dukwilma will receive six more inches in the next two days. That's more than the town usually gets in three months during this time of year. The students, like everyone else, are very concerned.

Underline.
If Dukwilma gets more rain, the following things could happen.
<u>The levee could break.</u>   The school could float away.   The students could go boating.
<u>The town could flood.</u>   Homes could be lost.   <u>Businesses could be lost.</u>

Check.
The effects of the rain could be devastating because . . .
- ☑ crops could be destroyed.
- ☑ businesses could be ruined.
- ☑ the town could shut down.
- ☐ the ground would be wet.
- ☐ people won't be able to use the river for fun.

Write.
If your house was in danger of being flooded and you had to evacuate, what would you do?
Answers will vary.

•SOMETHING EXTRA•
If your house was in danger of being flooded and you could take only three things with you, what would you take and why?

Page 38

Cassie's Dilemma

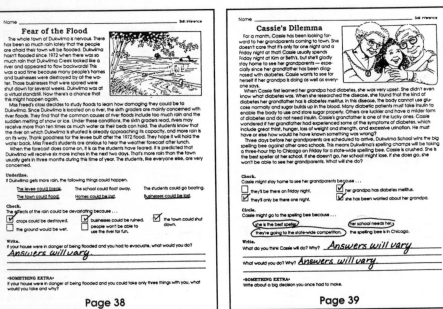

For a month, Cassie has been looking forward to her grandparents coming to town. She doesn't care that it's only for one night and a Friday night at that! Cassie usually spends Friday night at Kim or Beth's, but she'll gladly stay home to see her grandparents — especially since her grandfather has been diagnosed with diabetes. Cassie wants to see for herself if her grandpa is doing as well as everyone says.

When Cassie first learned her grandpa had diabetes, she was very upset. She didn't even know what diabetes was. When she researched the disease, she found that the kind of diabetes her grandfather has is diabetes mellitus. In this disease, the body cannot use glucose normally and sugar builds up in the blood. Many diabetic patients must take insulin to enable the body to use and store sugar properly. Others are luckier and have a milder form of diabetes and do not need insulin. Cassie's grandfather is one of the lucky ones. Cassie wondered if her grandfather had experienced some of the symptoms of diabetes, which include great thirst, hunger, loss of weight and strength, and excessive urination. He must have or else how would he have known something was wrong?

Three days before her grandparents are scheduled to arrive, Dukwilma School wins the big spelling bee against other area schools. This means Dukwilma's spelling champs will be taking a three-hour trip to Chicago on Friday for a state-wide spelling bee. Cassie is crushed. She is the best speller at the school. If she doesn't go, her school might lose. If she does go, she won't be able to see her grandparents. What will she do?

Check.
Cassie might stay home to see her grandparents because . . .
- ☐ they'll be there on Friday night.
- ☑ her grandpa has diabetes mellitus.
- ☐ they'll only be there for one night.
- ☑ she has been worried about her grandpa.

Circle.
Cassie might go to the spelling bee because . . .
(she is the best speller.)   (her school needs her.)
(they're going to the state-wide competition.)   the spelling bee is in Chicago.

Write.
What do you think Cassie will do? Why? *Answers will vary.*

What would you do? Why? *Answers will vary.*

•SOMETHING EXTRA•
Write about a big decision you once had to make.

Page 39

Will Kim Go On?

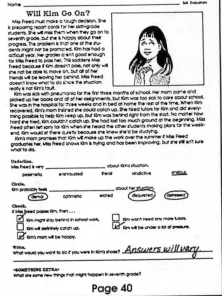

Miss Freed must make a tough decision. She is preparing report cards for her sixth-grade students. She will miss them when they go on to seventh grade, but she is happy about their progress. The problem is that one of the students might not be promoted. Kim has had a difficult year. Her grades aren't good enough for Miss Freed to pass her. This saddens Miss Freed because if Kim doesn't pass, not only will she not be able to move on, but all of her friends will be leaving her behind. Miss Freed doesn't know what to do since the situation really is not Kim's fault.

Kim was sick with pneumonia for the first three months of school. Her mom came and picked up her books and all of her assignments, but Kim was too sick to care about schoolwork. She was in the hospital for three weeks and in bed at home the rest of the time. When Kim recovered, she was behind. She could catch up. She hired tutors for Kim and did everything possible to help Kim keep up, but Kim was behind right from the start. No matter how hard she tried, Kim couldn't catch up. She had lost too much ground at the beginning. Miss Freed often felt sorry for Kim when she heard the other students making plans for the weekend. Kim would sit there quietly because she knew she'd be studying.

Kim's mom promises that Kim will make up the work over the summer if Miss Freed graduates her. Miss Freed knows Kim is trying and has been improving, but she still isn't sure what to do.

Underline.
Miss Freed is very _____ about Kim's situation.
pessimistic   <u>unnerved</u>   literal   vindictive   <u>anxious</u>

Circle.
Kim probably feels _____ about her situation.
(dismal)   optimistic   elated   (disquieted)   (depressed)

Check.
If Miss Freed passes Kim, then . . .
- ☑ Kim might stay behind in school work.
- ☐ Kim won't need any more tutors.
- ☐ Kim will definitely catch up.
- ☑ Kim will be under a lot of pressure.
- ☑ Kim's mom will be happy.

Write.
What would you want to do if you were in Kim's shoes? *Answers will vary.*

•SOMETHING EXTRA•
What are some new things that might happen in seventh grade?

Page 40

I Do, or I Don't?

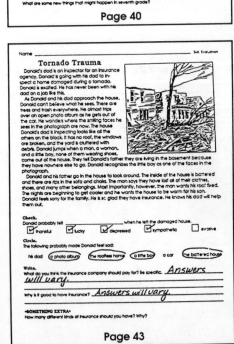

Sam Spacey asked Miss Freed to marry him! The sixth graders are all so excited. He asked her at Dukwilma Day in front of the whole school! The two were running a one-legged race together and were almost at the finish line when Sam tripped and they both fell. While they struggled to get up, Sam pulled a ring out of his pocket and in front of everyone asked Miss Freed to marry him. All the kids cheered as Sam put the ring on Miss Freed's finger. She stood there looking shocked.

The next day, Cassie, Maria, and Beth asked Miss Freed when the wedding would be. Miss Freed blushed and said very quietly to the girls that she hadn't made up her mind yet. The girls were amazed. What did they have to talk about? All they had to do was get married. Miss Freed explained there were many things they had to consider before getting married. For instance, they both own houses, so whose would they live in? Plus, Sam lives in Dailey and she lives in Dukwilma, so they also had to decide in which town to live. Miss Freed has a cat, and Sam is allergic to cats. What would happen to Hairy? And, Miss Freed wants at least two children, and Sam isn't sure he wants any. So, as Miss Freed explained, the two had some big decisions to make. The girls went out to play, leaving Miss Freed deep in thought.

Circle.
Marriage is not something you should . . .
do.   even think about.   (rush into.)   ever want.   (consider lightly.)

Check.
Miss Freed and Sam must discuss the following before setting a date:
- ☑ Hairy the cat
- ☑ where to live
- ☑ children
- ☐ Rover the dog
- ☐ what to buy
- ☐ a wedding dress

Underline.
Marriage is a big and important . . .
<u>step</u>   commitment   commandment   question.

Write.
List five things you should consider when you get married. *Answers will vary.*

•SOMETHING EXTRA•
What do you want to do after you graduate from high school?

Page 41

Who Will Win?

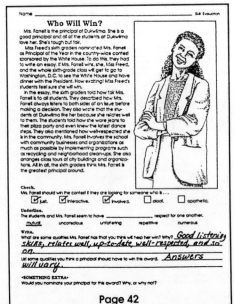

Mrs. Farrel is the principal of Dukwilma. She is a good principal and all of the students at Dukwilma love her. She's tough but fair.

Miss Freed's sixth graders nominated Mrs. Farrel as Principal of the Year in the country-wide contest sponsored by the White House. To do this, they had to write an essay. If Mrs. Farrel wins, she, Miss Freed, and the whole sixth-grade class will get to go to Washington, D.C. to see the White House and have dinner with the President. How exciting! Miss Freed's students feel sure she will win.

In the essay, the sixth graders told how fair Mrs. Farrel is to all students. They described how Mrs. Farrel always listens to both sides of an issue before making a decision. They also wrote that the students at Dukwilma like her because she relates well to them. The students told how she wore jeans to their pizza party and even knew the latest dance steps. They also mentioned how well-respected she is in the community. Mrs. Farrel involves the school with community businesses and organizations as much as possible by implementing programs such as recycling and neighborhood clean-ups. She also arranges class tours of city buildings and organizations. All in all, the sixth graders think Mrs. Farrel is the greatest principal around.

Check.
Mrs. Farrel should win the contest if they are looking for someone who is . . .
- ☑ just.
- ☑ interactive.
- ☑ involved.
- ☐ aloof.
- ☐ apathetic.

Underline.
The students and Mrs. Farrel seem to have _____ respect for one another.
<u>mutual</u>   unconscious   unfaltering   repetitive   numerous

Write.
What are some qualities that Mrs. Farrel has that you think will help her win? Why? *Good listening skills, relates well, up-to-date, well-respected, and so on.*

List some qualities you think a principal should have to win the award. *Answers will vary.*

•SOMETHING EXTRA•
Would you nominate your principal for the award? Why, or why not?

Page 42

Tornado Trauma

Donald's dad is an inspector for an insurance agency. Donald is going with his dad to inspect a home damaged during a tornado. Donald is excited. He has never been with his dad on a job like this.

As Donald and his dad approach the house, Donald can't believe what he sees. There are trees and trash everywhere. He almost trips over an open photo album as he gets out of the car. He wonders where the smiling faces he sees in the photograph are now. The house Donald's dad is inspecting looks like all the others on the block. It has no roof, the windows are broken, and the yard is cluttered with debris. Donald jumps when a man, a woman, and a little boy, none of them wearing shoes, come out of the house. They tell Donald's father they are living in the basement because they have nowhere else to go. Donald recognizes the little boy as one of the faces in the photograph.

Donald and his father go in the house to look around. The inside of the house is battered and there are rips in the sofa and chairs. The man says they have lost all of their clothes, shoes, and many other belongings. Most importantly, however, the man wants his roof fixed. The nights are beginning to get cooler and he wants the house to be warm for his son. Donald feels sorry for the family. He is so glad they have insurance. He knows his dad will help them out.

Check.
Donald probably felt _____ when he left the damaged house.
- ☑ thankful
- ☑ lucky
- ☑ depressed
- ☑ sympathetic
- ☐ evasive

Circle.
The following probably made Donald feel sad:
his dad   (a photo album)   (the roofless home)   (a little boy)   a car   (the battered house)

Write.
What do you think the insurance company should pay for? Be specific. *Answers will vary.*

Why is it good to have insurance? *Answers will vary.*

•SOMETHING EXTRA•
How many different kinds of insurance should you have? Why?

Page 43
